BrightRED Study Guide

Curriculum for Excellence

N5

MUSIC

Adrian Finnerty

First published in 2017 by:
Bright Red Publishing Ltd
1 Torphichen Street
Edinburgh
EH3 8HX

Copyright © Bright Red Publishing Ltd 2017

Cover image © Caleb Rutherford

All rights reserved. No part of this publication may be reproduced, stored in a retrieval system, or transmitted in any form or by any means, electronic, mechanical, photocopying, recording or otherwise, without prior permission in writing from the publisher.

The rights of Adrian Finnerty to be identified as the author of this work has been asserted by him in accordance with Sections 77 and 78 of the Copyright, Designs and Patents Act 1988.

A CIP record for this book is available from the British Library.

ISBN 978-1-906736-86-6

With thanks to:
Sue Lyons (editorial) and PDQ Digital Media Solutions (layout)
Cover design and series book design by Caleb Rutherford – e i d e t i c.

Acknowledgements
Every effort has been made to seek all copyright-holders. If any have been overlooked, then Bright Red Publishing will be delighted to make the necessary arrangements.

Permission has been sought from all relevant copyright holders and Bright Red Publishing are grateful for the use of the following:

The Dark Island. Words by David Silver & music by Iain Maclachlan © Copyright 1963 Essex Music Limited. Transferred 1967 to Westminster Music Limited, Suite 2.07, Plaza 535 Kings Road, London SW10 0SZ for the World. All Rights Reserved. International Copyright Secured. Used by permission of Music Sales Limited.

Images licensed by Ingram Image on pages 10, 12, 19, 20, 21, 25, 28, 29, 31, 33, 34, 35, 36, 40, 41, 42, 43, 44, 45, 54, 46, 47, 48, 49, 54, 56, 57, 79, 80, 81, 83, 87, 88, 89, 90, 91; Public domain images on pages 12, 25, 26, 27, 28, 46, 57, 62; Lukassek/iStock.com (p 6); adil113 (CC BY 2.0)[3] (p 8); Kirill_Liv/iStock.com (p 8); Michael Coghlan (CC BY-SA 2.0)[2] (p 8); Bryan Ledgard (CC BY 2.0)[3] (p 9); Ishikawa Ken (CC BY-SA 2.0)[2] (p 10); Caleb Rutherford – e i d e t i c (p 10); candyschwartz (CC BY 2.0)[3] (p 11); USDA photo by Steve Thompson (CC BY 2.0)[3] (p 18); Caleb Rutherford – e i d e t i c (p 19); Vladimir Morozov (CC BY 2.0)[3] (pp 20 and 47); Rog01 (CC BY-SA 2.0)[2] (p 20); Daniel Stockman (CC BY-SA 2.0)[2] (p 21); Caleb Rutherford – e i d e t i c (p 21); S Limbért (CC BY-ND 2.0)[4] (p 25); Hans Bernhard (Schnobby) (CC BY-SA 3.0)[1] (p 26); Ky (CC BY 2.0)[3] (p 26); guyman22 (CC BY 2.0)[3] (p 27); Caleb Rutherford – e i d e t i c (p 28); julio zeppelin (CC BY-ND 2.0)[4] (p 29); Piotr Drabik (CC BY 2.0)[3] (p 30); Daisuke FUJII (CC BY 2.0)[3] (p 37); Torekhan Sarmanov (CC BY 2.0)[3] (p 37); DragonImages/iStock.com (p 39); Sissih292 (CC BY-SA 4.0)[5] (p 40); Yamaha Corporation (CC BY-SA 4.0)[5] (p 41); sutteerug (p 44); Allanbeavis (CC BY-SA 3.0)[1] (p 44); Alexandre Delbos (CC BY 2.0)[3] (p 45); adil113 (CC BY 2.0)[3] (p 46); Hannes Grobe (CC BY-SA 3.0)[1] (p 47); Ukrphoto/Dreamstime (p 48); FREYmanagement (CC BY-SA 3.0)[1] (p 52); Caleb Rutherford – e i d e t i c (p 61); Caleb Rutherford – e i d e t i c (p 65); Christopher-Oliver/iStock.com (p 81); SteveAllenPhoto/iStock.com (p 92).

[1] (CC BY-SA 3.0) https://creativecommons.org/licenses/by-sa/3.0/
[2] (CC BY-SA 2.0) https://creativecommons.org/licenses/by-sa/2.0/
[3] (CC BY 2.0) https://creativecommons.org/licenses/by/2.0/
[4] (CC BY-ND 2.0) https://creativecommons.org/licenses/by-nd/2.0/
[5] (CC BY-SA 4.0) https://creativecommons.org/licenses/by-sa/4.0/

Printed and bound in the UK by Ashford Colour Ltd.

NATIONAL 5 MUSIC STUDY GUIDE

INTRODUCTION
Course overview 4

THE MUSIC OF SCOTLAND
Scottish dances and instrumental forms 6
Instruments 1 8
Instruments 2 10
Scottish vocal music 12
Composing – melody, harmony and rhythm 14
Composing a Scottish waltz 16

WORLD MUSIC
Caribbean, Indian and South American music 18
Latin American, Spanish and African music 20
Composing in a Latin American or Calypso style .. 22

POPULAR MUSIC
Blues, Gospel and Ragtime 24
Jazz and Swing 26
Rock'n'roll, Rock, Pop, Reggae, Celtic Rock and Rap 28
Composing popular music 1 30
Composing popular music 2 32

VOCAL MUSIC
Types of voices 34
Choral music, musicals and opera 36
Word setting, song structure and backing vocals .. 38

TIMBRE – INSTRUMENTS AND HOW THEY ARE PLAYED
Instruments of the orchestra: woodwind 40
Instruments of the orchestra: brass 42
Instruments of the orchestra: strings 44
Instruments of the orchestra: percussion 46
Keyboards and guitars 48

FORMS, STYLES AND PERIODS
Musical forms 50
Baroque music 1 52
Baroque music 2 54
Classical music 1 56
Classical music 2 58
Romantic music 60

TWENTIETH-CENTURY MUSIC
Impressionist music 62
Minimalist music 64

MUSIC LITERACY
Concepts and melody/harmony 66
More on melody/harmony 68
Rhythm/tempo and timbre/dynamics 70

COURSE ASSESSMENT
Question paper 72
More on the question paper 74
More question styles 76
Composing assignment 1 78
Composing assignment 2 80
Composing assignment 3 82
Composing assignment 4 84
Performance 1 86
Performance 2 88
Performance 3 90
Performance 4 92

GLOSSARY OF CONCEPTS 94

INTRODUCTION

COURSE OVERVIEW

INTRODUCTION

The aims of the National 5 Music course overall are to enable you to:

- broaden your knowledge and understanding of music and musical literacy by listening to music and learning to recognise, and distinguish, level-specific music concepts, signs and symbols used in music notation
- experiment with, and use, music concepts in creative ways, using compositional methods to compose original music and self-reflect on your creative choices
- develop performing skills on two instruments, or one instrument and voice, through regular practice and self-reflection.

Throughout the National 5 Music course you will develop a range of musical skills, knowledge and understanding. These will include:

- skills in listening to music to promote aural perception and discrimination
- knowledge and understanding of music styles, concepts, notation signs and symbols
- skills in creating original music using compositional methods
- reviewing the creative process and evaluating your own composing
- skills in performing music in contrasting styles on two contrasting instruments, or one instrument and voice
- self-reflection and review of your rehearsal and practice skills.

COURSE CONTENT

The National 5 Music course has an integrated approach to learning about music. It combines practical activities in performing and composing with music literacy and listening to music. Learning about a wide range of music concepts is central to the course. Throughout the course, you will have opportunities to draw upon your understanding of music styles and concepts as you experiment with these in creative ways when performing and creating music.

National 5 Music concepts

The music concepts are all the styles, music features and terms that you will learn about as part of your National 5 Music course. You will explore these concepts in a variety of ways through listening to music, creating your own music and performing music.

The concepts in the National 5 Music course build on previous knowledge and understanding of music concepts at lower levels. This means that you will be expected to have a secure understanding of the music concepts at National 3 and National 4 levels, in addition to knowledge and understanding of the National 5 music concepts.

The three tables shown list all the concepts that you will be required to know for National 3, National 4 and National 5 Music.

Styles	Melody/harmony	Rhythm/tempo	Texture/structure/form	Timbre/dynamics

Blues
Jazz
Rock
Pop
Rock'n'roll
Musical
Scottish
Latin American
	Ascending
	Descending
	Step (stepwise)
	Leap (leaping)
	Repetition
	Sequence
	Question and answer
	Improvisation
	Chord
	Discord
	Chord change
		Accent/accented
		Beat/pulse
		Bar
		2, 3 or 4 beats in the bar
		On the beat/off the beat
		Repetition
		Slower/faster
		Pause
		March
		Reel
		Waltz
		Drum fill
		Adagio
		Allegro
			Unison/octave
			Harmony/chord
			Solo
			Accompanied
			Unaccompanied
			Repetition
			Ostinato
			Riff
			Round
				Striking (hitting)
				Blowing
				Bowing
				Strumming
				Plucking
				Orchestra:
				  Woodwind
				  Brass
				  Percussion (tuned and untuned)
				  Strings
				Accordion
				Fiddle
				Bagpipes
				Acoustic guitar
				Electric guitar
				Piano
				Organ
				Drum kit
				Steel band
				Scottish dance band
				Folk group
				Voice
				Choir
				Staccato
				Legato

Music literacy				
Lines and spaces of the treble clef Steps Repetition		Crotchet Minim Dotted minim Semibreve Barlines Double barlines		*f* – forte *p* – piano *cresc* – crescendo *dim* – diminuendo

Music concepts **National 3**

contd

Introduction – Course overview

Styles	Melody/harmony	Rhythm/tempo	Texture/structure/form	Timbre/dynamics

Baroque
Ragtime
Romantic
Swing
Concerto
Opera
Scots ballads
Mouth music
Reggae
African music
Rapping
	Major/minor (tonality)
	Drone
	Broken chord
	Arpeggio
	Chord progression (chords I, IV and V in major keys)
	Change of key
	Pedal
	Scale
	Pentatonic scale
	Octave
	Vamp
	Scat singing
	Ornament
		Syncopation
		Scotch snap
		Strathspey
		Jig
		Simple time:
		  2 3 4
		  4 4 4
		Compound time
		Anacrusis
		Andante
		Accelerando
		Rallentando
		A tempo
		Dotted rhythms
			Canon
			Ternary (ABA)
			Verse and chorus
			Middle 8
			Theme and variation
			Cadenza
			Imitation
				Brass band
				Wind band
				Violin
				Cello
				Double bass
				Harp
				Flute
				Clarinet
				Saxophone
				Pan pipes
				Recorder
				Trumpet
				Trombone
				Timpani
				Snare drum
				Bass drum
				Cymbals
				Triangle
				Tambourine
				Guiro
				Xylophone
				Glockenspiel
				Harpsichord
				Bass guitar
				Distortion
				Muted
				Soprano
				Alto
				Tenor
				Bass
				Backing vocals

Music literacy				
Treble clef stave C–A′ sequences		Quaver Semiquaver Grouped semiquavers Paired quavers Repeat signs		*mf* – mezzo forte *mp* – mezzo piano

Music concepts **National 4**

Styles	Melody/harmony	Rhythm/tempo	Texture/structure/form	Timbre/dynamics

Symphony
Gospel
Classical
Pibroch
Celtic rock
Bothy ballad
Waulking song
Gaelic psalm
Aria
Chorus
Minimalist
Indian
	Atonal
	Cluster
	Chord progression (I, IV, V, VI in major keys)
	Imperfect/perfect cadences
	Inverted pedal
	Chromatic
	Whole-tone scale
	Grace note
	Glissando
	Modulation
	Contrary motion
	Trill
	Syllabic
	Melismatic
	Countermelody
	Descant (voice)
	Pitch bend
	Tone/semitone
		Rubato
		Ritardando
		Moderato
		Cross rhythms
		Compound time:
		  6 9 12
		  8 8 8
			Strophic
			Binary (AB)
			Rondo (ABACA...)
			Episode
			Alberti bass
			Walking bass
			Ground bass
			Homophonic
			Polyphonic
			Contrapuntal
			Coda
				Piccolo
				Oboe
				Bassoon
				(French) horn
				Tuba
				Viola
				Castanets
				Hi-hat cymbals
				Bongo drums
				Clarsach
				Bodhrán
				Sitar
				Tabla
				Arco
				Pizzicato
				Con sordino
				Flutter tonguing
				Rolls
				Reverb
				Mezzo-soprano
				Baritone
				A cappella

Music literacy				
	Tones Semitones Accidentals (flats, sharps and naturals) Scales and key signatures (C major, G major, F major and A minor) Chords (C major, G major, F major and A minor) Leaps	Dotted rhythms Dotted crotchet Dotted quaver Scotch snap First and second time bars		*ff* – fortissimo *pp* – pianissimo *sfz* – sforzando

Music Concepts **National 5**

THINGS TO DO AND THINK ABOUT

For the National 5 Music course, you will need to know all the music concepts for National 3, National 4 and National 5.

Create a mind map for each theme or topic that you study, showing which concepts relate to that theme.

ONLINE

Performance self-reflection sheets and composing review sheets are available at www.brightredbooks.net

ONLINE

The answers for all the activities in this book, along with many other resources, can be found at www.brightredbooks.net

THE MUSIC OF SCOTLAND

SCOTTISH DANCES AND INSTRUMENTAL FORMS

This area of work covers the most important musical features and concepts associated with **Scottish music**. It will involve listening to, performing, and composing music.

BACKGROUND

Music and dance have always been an important part of Scottish culture. Music has often been used for:

- special occasions such as weddings or funerals
- accompanying work in the tweed mills or on the farms
- ceilidhs, where people would dance, sing songs and tell stories.

SCOTTISH DANCES AND INSTRUMENTAL FORMS

There are a number of different dances and instrumental forms, including:

- waltz
- march
- strathspey
- reel
- jig.

Waltz	A dance with 3 beats in the bar.

EXAMPLE:

The Dark Island is an example of a waltz. Although regarded by many as a traditional Scottish song, it was composed by Iain MacLachlan as the theme to a 1962 television series called *The Dark Island*, set on the island of Benbecula in the Outer Hebrides.

Look out for the following musical features in *The Dark Island*:

- key signature of F♯, indicating the key of G major
- time signature indicating 3 beats in the bar
- dotted rhythms (dotted crotchet followed by a quaver)
- the melody begins with an anacrusis (upbeat).

March	A piece of music with 2 or 4 beats in the bar, originally composed for soldiers to march to.

EXAMPLE:

Scotland the Brave is an example of a march.

Look out for the following musical features in *Scotland the Brave*:

- key signature with no flats or sharps, indicating the key of C major
- time signature indicating 4 beats in the bar
- dotted rhythms (a dotted quaver followed by a semiquaver) on the second beat of every bar

---

VIDEO LINK

Listen to examples of: a Scottish waltz; a march; a strathspey; a reel and a jig at www.brightredbooks.net/N5Music

DON'T FORGET

The key signatures of both C major and A minor have no sharps or flats. However, in the key of A minor you would expect to see some G sharps as accidentals. In most of the bars of *Scotland the Brave*, the notes happen to outline the chord of C major. Also, if you play or listen to this melody, it ends on the note C and sounds major.

ONLINE

Learn more about Scottish dances at www.brightredbooks.net/N5Music

contd

The music of Scotland – Scottish dances and instrumental forms

- the melody begins on the first beat of the bar
- 1st and 2nd time endings.

Strathspey	A Scottish dance characterised by dotted rhythms. The strathspey usually features the Scotch snap (a short note on the beat followed by a long note).

Dotted rhythm **Scotch snap**

EXAMPLE:

Tullochgorum is an example of a strathspey.

Look out for the following musical features in *Tullochgorum*:

- key signature of F#, indicating the key of G major
- time signature indicating 4 beats in the bar
- accidentals (notice the frequent use of F♮)
- dotted rhythms and Scotch snaps
- the melody begins with an anacrusis (upbeat)
- the music should be played at a reasonably slow tempo.

Reel	A fast Scottish dance in either 2/4 or 4/4 time. A reel generally features an even flowing rhythm and is usually played after a strathspey.

EXAMPLE:

The Flowers of Edinburgh is an example of a reel.

Look out for the following musical features in *The Flowers of Edinburgh*:

- key signature of B♭, indicating the key of F major
- time signature indicating 4 beats in the bar
- the melody begins with an anacrusis (upbeat)
- even flowing quavers
- the music should be played at a reasonably fast tempo.

Jig	A fast dance in compound time. A jig is often written in 6/8, 9/8 or 12/8.

In compound time, the beat is a dotted note which divides into three.

For example, 6/8 = two dotted crotchet beats in a bar and each beat can be divided into three quavers.

EXAMPLE:

The Maid on the Green is an example of a jig.

Look out for the following musical features in *The Maid on the Green*:

- key signature of F#, indicating the key of G major
- time signature indicating 6/8 time (an example of compound time)
- the melody begins with an anacrusis (upbeat)
- the music should be played at a fast tempo.

DON'T FORGET

- A waltz is a dance with 3 beats in a bar.
- A march has a feeling of either 2 or 4 beats in a bar.
- A strathspey is a relatively slow dance, featuring dotted rhythms and Scotch snaps.
- A reel is a fast dance with even flowing quavers.
- A jig is a fast dance in compound time (i.e. 6/8, 9/8 or 12/8).

ONLINE TEST

Test yourself on Scottish dances and instrumental forms at www.brightredbooks.net/N5Music

THE MUSIC OF SCOTLAND

INSTRUMENTS 1

There are a number of instruments which, although played around the world, are often associated with Scotland in particular.

Some of the most common are:

- bagpipes
- fiddle
- accordion
- clarsach
- bodhrán
- whistle.

1. Chanter 2. Bag 3. Stock 4. Blowpipe 5. Tenor drones 6. Bass drone 7. Tuning slide 8. Cords

BAGPIPES

There are two main types of bagpipes that are common to Scotland: the Great Highland bagpipe and the Lowland bagpipe.

Highland bagpipes

Although originally from Scotland, the Highland bagpipes have gained popularity all over the world.

The instrument consists of:

- Bag – this was originally made from animal skin but is now more commonly made from synthetic materials. This provides a steady flow of air while playing the music.
- Mouthpiece and blowpipe – for the player to blow into.
- Chanter – a pipe played with two hands and containing a double reed. The chanter can play the following nine notes:

- Reeds – there is a double reed (like that of an oboe) at the top of the chanter and there are single reeds for the drones.
- Drones – there are generally three drones: two tenor drones and one bass drone (which plays an octave below). The drones produce a continuous note in the background while the melody is played on the chanter.

VIDEO LINK

Listen to the Highland and Lowland bagpipes at www.brightredbooks.net/N5Music

Drones

Drones are the low-pitched pipes of bagpipes which play a continuous note in the background to accompany the melody.

The term **drone** also describes a note, or notes, held or repeated in a piece of music.

Lowland bagpipes

One of the main differences between the Lowland and Highland bagpipes is that the Lowland pipes have a small bellow that provides the instrument with air. It has two drones (tenor and bass) and is much quieter than the Highland bagpipes. This makes it a popular choice for Scottish dance bands and for indoor use.

In each case, listen out for the drone – the long (sustained) note in the background that you can still hear while the melody is playing.

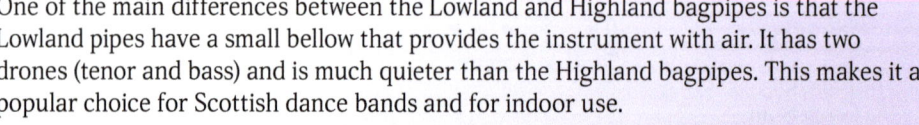

Bagpipes and side drum

Pipe band

In Scottish music, the bagpipes and drums make up a **pipe band**. Bagpipes were banned in Scotland in 1560 after the Reformation. It has also been suggested that they were banned again in 1747 after the Battle of Culloden. However, this has been a matter of debate.

contd

The music of Scotland – Instruments 1

Grace notes

An important characteristic of bagpipe music is the use of melodic ornamentation, including **grace notes**. These are short notes used to embellish the melody.

EXAMPLE:

Here is the melody of the *Skye Boat Song*, showing some characteristic bagpipe ornamentation:

The music of the bagpipes generally falls into two categories:

- Marches, jigs, strathspeys and reels. This is known as *Ceol Beag* (meaning light music in Gaelic).
- **Pibroch**. This is the *classical* music of the bagpipes and is known as *Ceol Mhor* (meaning great music in Gaelic).

A **Pibroch** is a theme and variations, with the variations becoming increasingly elaborate. The theme is usually a simple melody, called the *ground* or, in Gaelic, the *ùrlar*. The variations following the ground use different melodic embellishments, such as grace notes, which usually start simply and become more complex, before returning to the ground.

EXAMPLE:

Here is part of the Pibroch tune *Catherine's Lament* showing the ornamentation that is characteristic of the style:

FIDDLE

The **fiddle** is just another name for the violin, but the technique used by traditional music players is different to that of so-called classical players. This is mainly due to the ornamentation in the music, which varies from one part of the country to another. The repertoire for the fiddle comes from areas all around Scotland. Music from each of the areas has its own characteristics. Shetland fiddle music, for example, is different from Aberdeenshire fiddle music.

Famous Scots fiddle player Aly Bain

THINGS TO DO AND THINK ABOUT

1. What two types of music do the bagpipes generally play?
2. Which concept describes the long note held in the background while the melody is played on the bagpipes?
3. What type of dance is in compound time?
4. What are the main differences between a strathspey and a reel?

VIDEO LINK

Listen to a pipe band playing at www.brightredbooks.net/N5Music

VIDEO LINK

Listen to an example of the *Skye Boat Song*, and other tunes, being played by the bagpipes at www.brightredbooks.net/N5Music

VIDEO LINK

You can listen to the Pibroch tune *You're a Sly One* at www.brightredbooks.net/N5Music

DON'T FORGET

In the National 5 question paper, you may be required to identify bagpipes, a pipe band or Pibroch. However, you will not be required to tell the difference between the Highland bagpipes and the Lowland bagpipes.

VIDEO LINK

Listen to Aly Bain playing some Scots fiddle music at www.brightredbooks.net/N5Music

ONLINE TEST

Test yourself on Scottish instruments at www.brightredbooks.net/N5Music

THE MUSIC OF SCOTLAND

INSTRUMENTS 2

VIDEO LINK

Listen to an example of the clarsach being played at www.brightredbooks.net/N5Music

CLARSACH

The **clarsach** (Gaelic for *sounding strings*) is a small harp consisting of around 30 strings, which are colour-coded. The strings are made from gut and are tuned individually with a key. The clarsach has small levers at the top of each string that adjusts the pitch of each note by a semitone.

VIDEO LINK

Listen to the bodhrán being played at www.brightredbooks.net/N5Music

BODHRÁN

The **bodhrán** is a large hand-held drum that is often found in Scottish dance bands and traditional music groups. Bodhráns are often highly decorated and are played with a small double-ended beater or stick.

VIDEO LINK

Listen to an example of a whistle and a bodhrán being played at www.brightredbooks.net/N5Music

THE WHISTLE

The **whistle**, or tin whistle, is usually made from metal and is played at the front of the musician (like the recorder).

ACCORDION

The **accordion** has a small keyboard on one side (where the accordionist plays the melody with their right hand) and small buttons on the other side (enabling the accordionist to play chords with their left hand). Each button produces a major or minor chord. The bellows (also operated by the player's left hand) cause the air to flow, which produces the sound by making the reeds inside the body of the instrument vibrate. As well as being a popular solo instrument, the accordion is commonly found in Scottish dance bands.

VIDEO LINK

Listen to a solo accordion being played at www.brightredbooks.net/N5Music

The music of Scotland – Instruments 2

SCOTTISH DANCE BAND

A **Scottish dance band** is a group of musicians playing Scottish dances and songs on instruments such as the fiddle, accordion, piano, bass and drum kit.

A Scottish dance band is sometimes known as a **ceilidh band**, as they often play the music for ceilidh dances.

In Scottish traditional music, the piano often plays a simple accompaniment known as a **vamp**. This is a rhythmic accompaniment with a low note played by the left hand (**on the beat**) and a chord played by the right hand (**off the beat**). This type of piano accompaniment is often featured in music performed by Scottish dance bands.

VIDEO LINK
Listen to a Scottish dance band at www.brightredbooks.net/N5Music

VIDEO LINK
Listen to an example of a vamp at www.brightredbooks.net/N5Music

ONLINE
Learn more about Scottish instruments at www.brightredbooks.net/N5Music

ONLINE TEST
Test yourself on Scottish instruments at www.brightredbooks.net/N5Music

THINGS TO DO AND THINK ABOUT

1. Make a list of some instruments that are commonly associated with Scottish music.
2. Which instruments would you commonly find in a Scottish dance band?
3. Listen to examples of the different instruments associated with Scottish music so that you are confident about being able to identify them.

THE MUSIC OF SCOTLAND
SCOTTISH VOCAL MUSIC

MOUTH MUSIC

Mouth music is a very rhythmical style of singing, with Gaelic or nonsense words. It has traditionally been used for ceilidh dancing when no instruments were available. Mouth music would generally have been unaccompanied, although in modern performances it is not uncommon to have some kind of instrumental accompaniment, possibly provided by the **bodhrán**. Some elements of mouth music may have originated as memory aids for, or alternatives to, instrumental music such as bagpipe tunes.

VIDEO LINK

Listen to an example of mouth music at www.brightredbooks.net/N5Music

WAULKING SONG

Much of the music composed in Scotland was for a specific purpose or special occasion. Many songs were composed to accompany work.

One of the most common forms of work-song was the **waulking song**. Waulking was the process of shrinking tweed by wetting the tweed, then thumping it on a board, which made the tweed stronger and more waterproof. This work was traditionally carried out by women. The waulking songs were very rhythmic, with strong accents (to accompany the thumping of the tweed) and often in a call and response style (i.e. the soloist and group would alternate).

SCOTS BALLAD

A ballad is a song that tells a story. Ballads are often quite long (in comparison with other songs) and generally have several **verses**. They are usually **strophic** in form (i.e. they have the same music for every verse). Some ballads also have a **chorus** (a repeated section of the song that would have the same words and music each time) that comes in between the verses. **Scots ballads** were often composed to tell the stories of historical events, places or people associated with Scotland. Examples of Scots ballads include *The Braes o' Killiecrankie* and *The Massacre of Glencoe*.

VIDEO LINK

Listen to an example of a waulking song at www.brightredbooks.net/N5Music

BOTHY BALLAD

As well as songs for work, there were also songs about work. An example of this is the **bothy ballad**. A farm bothy was a small dwelling in the north-east of Scotland where farm workers lived while working on the farms. Traditionally sung by men, bothy ballads were songs about the farm, the work, the farmer himself or the poor conditions the farm workers lived in. They would generally be sung unaccompanied.

VIDEO LINK

Listen to The Corries singing *The Massacre of Glencoe* at www.brightredbooks.net/N5Music

EXAMPLE:

The Muckin' o' Geordie's Byre

At a relic aul' croft upon the hill,
Roon the neuk frae Sprottie's mill,
Tryin' a' his life tae jine the kill
Lived Geordie MacIntyre.
He had a wife a swir's himsel'
An' a daughter as black's auld Nick himsel',
There wis some fun-haud awa' the smell
At the muckin' o' Geordie's byre.

The music of Scotland – Scottish vocal music

GAELIC PSALM

A psalm is a musical setting of a text from the bible. The Gaelic churches, particularly in the Western Isles of Scotland, have their own distinct way of singing psalm tunes. These are still used in some areas today. When the psalms were originally introduced, few people would have been able to read music and there would have been very few copies of the words. Therefore, the first couple of lines would have been sung by one person who led the singing (known as the Precentor), then the congregation would join in singing their own individual interpretations of the melody, adding their own ornamentation (extra notes in the melody). The psalms are often very slow, and generally unaccompanied.

VIDEO LINK

Listen to examples of bothy ballads at www.brightredbooks.net/N5Music

CELTIC ROCK

This is a style of music that mixes folk or traditional music with rock music.

In the 1970s, the group Runrig produced music that is often described as a blend of folk and rock music. The lyrics of the songs often focus on Scottish locations, history, politics or people. Some songs also make references to agriculture and land conservation.

In the 1980s, the group Capercaillie combined Scottish folk music with traditional Gaelic songs and modern songs. They often mixed Gaelic songs and music with modern production techniques, combining traditional lyrics and tunes with modern techniques and instruments such as synthesisers, drum machines, electric guitars and bass guitars.

VIDEO LINK

Listen to examples of Gaelic psalm singing at www.brightredbooks.net/N5Music

DON'T FORGET

Remember that waulking songs would have traditionally been sung by women, whereas the bothy ballads would have been sung by men. Mouth music uses nonsense words while Gaelic psalms are religious pieces. Scots ballads tell the stories of historical events, places or people associated with Scotland.

ACTIVITY

Listen to *Toss the Feathers* by The Corrs at www.brightredbooks.net/N5Music.

As you listen, try to identify the following:

- the instruments being played by the members of the group
- which aspects of the music are traditional or folk-like
- which aspects of the music are more like Rock or Pop?

ONLINE

Learn more about bothy ballads at www.brightredbooks.net/N5Music

THINGS TO DO AND THINK ABOUT

1. Make a list of the different styles associated with Scottish vocal music.
2. Identify some of the important features of each type of Scottish vocal music.
3. Listen to examples of the different types of Scottish vocal music so that you are confident that you are able to identify them.

ONLINE TEST

Test yourself on Scottish vocal music at www.brightredbooks.net/N5Music

THE MUSIC OF SCOTLAND

COMPOSING – MELODY, HARMONY AND RHYTHM

There are a number of melodic, harmonic and rhythmic features that commonly appear in Scottish music. These are features that you should try to include in your composing assignment.

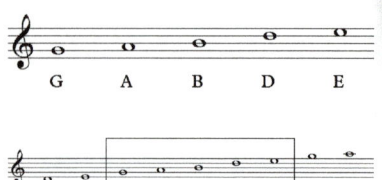

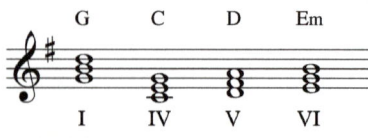

MELODY

A common feature of many Scottish songs is the use of the **pentatonic scale.** This is a scale containing five notes. The notes of the pentatonic scale starting on G are G, A, B, D and E.

Although there are only five notes in the pentatonic scale, it is perfectly acceptable to use the same notes either an octave higher or an octave lower.

HARMONY

The four most common chords that can be used in the key of G major, to accompany a melody, are G, C, D, and E minor.

The table lists the chord number, the chord name, and the three notes contained in each chord.

Chord number	Chord name	Notes contained in the chord
I	G	G, B and D
IV	C	C, E and G
V	D	D, F sharp and A
VI	Em (E minor)	E, G and B

RHYTHM

Scottish songs and dances are either in **simple time** or **compound time**, depending on the particular dance.

Simple time

In simple time each beat can be divided into two.

Here is part of the *Uist Tramping Song*. It has a time signature of 4/4, which is an example of simple time. The melody begins with an **anacrusis (upbeat)** and contains examples of **dotted rhythms** (a **dotted quaver** followed by a **semiquaver**). The melody also uses only the notes of the **pentatonic scale**.

EXAMPLE: *Uist Tramping Song*

ONLINE

Head to www.brightredbooks.net/N5Music for an extra activity.

ONLINE TEST

Test yourself on melody and rhythm at www.brightredbooks.net/N5Music

Here is part of the tune *Ye Banks and Braes*. It has a time signature of 3/4, which is also an example of **simple time**. The melody also begins with an anacrusis (upbeat). Notice that this part of the melody also uses the notes of the **pentatonic scale**.

EXAMPLE: *Ye Banks and Braes*

contd

Compound time

Compound time is when the beat can be divided into three. **Jigs** are always in compound time.

Here is part of the tune *The Wee Cooper o' Fife*. This has a time signature of 6/8 which means that there are two dotted crotchet beats in every bar. Each dotted crotchet beat can be divided into three quavers. This means that *The Wee Cooper o' Fife* is in compound time.

EXAMPLE: *The Wee Cooper o' Fife*

ACTIVITY: Ye Banks and Braes – A Scottish waltz

Ye Banks and Braes is an example of a **Scottish waltz**. The music is in **ternary form**. This means that it has three sections: **A**, **B** and **A** repeated.

Section A: The first line has the main part of the melody. It starts with an anacrusis and ends with an **imperfect cadence** (i.e. it ends on **chord V** which creates an 'unfinished' effect). The second line is almost a repeat of the first line, but ends on a **perfect cadence** (i.e. **chord V** followed by **chord I**, which makes the music sound 'finished').

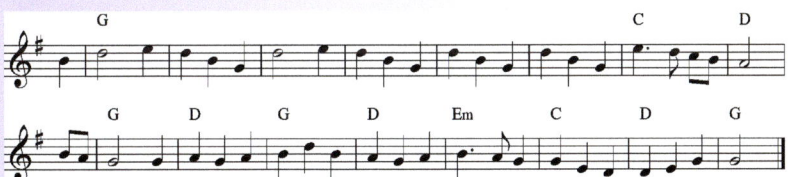

Section B: The second section is shorter and provides some contrast. There is quite a bit of repetition in bars 4, 5 and 6 of this section, and it ends on an imperfect cadence, making it sound unfinished.

Section A(2): This is a repeat of the second half of the first section, making the melody sound complete.

THINGS TO DO AND THINK ABOUT

Having played and analysed the melody of *Ye Banks and Braes*, you should now answer the following questions:

1. What is the **time signature** of *Ye Banks and Braes*?
2. Is this an example of simple time or compound time?
3. Which concept describes the rhythm at the very beginning of the melody?
4. Which concept describes the overall structure/form of the music?
5. What type of cadence do both the first and third phrases end with?
6. What type of cadence do both the second and fourth phrases end with?
7. What is the letter name of the highest note in the music?
8. How many beats does the final note last for?

DON'T FORGET
A waltz has three beats in every bar.

DON'T FORGET
A jig is in compound time.

DON'T FORGET
An anacrusis is when the melody does not begin on the first beat of the bar.

DON'T FORGET
A dotted rhythm features a longer note followed by a shorter note:

DON'T FORGET
A scotch snap features a shorter note followed by a longer note:

DON'T FORGET
A pentatonic scale contains five notes.

DON'T FORGET
Chords I, IV and V in a major key are all major chords. Chord VI is a minor chord.

DON'T FORGET
A cadence consists of two chords. A **perfect cadence** is formed by chord V followed by chord I and sounds 'finished'. An **imperfect cadence** is formed by any chord followed by chord V, creating an 'unfinished' effect.

THE MUSIC OF SCOTLAND
COMPOSING A SCOTTISH WALTZ

MELODY

You are going to compose a melody in the style of a **Scottish waltz**. To do this you will need to make sure that you know what musical features you would expect to find in a Scottish waltz.

For your own melody, you should use the notes of the **pentatonic scale** based on **G**.

These notes are G, A, B, D and E.

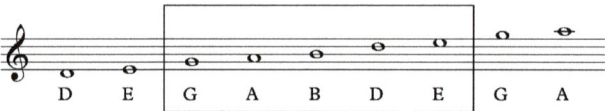

Try playing the notes of this scale on your chosen instrument. Get to know the notes well. Then, experiment by varying the order of the notes to try and make more interesting patterns of notes.

Experiment with the following **melodic** concepts:

ascending	descending	repetition
Moving by **step**	Moving by **leap**	Sequence

Then experiment with the following **rhythmic** features:

dotted rhythms	scotch snaps	repeated rhythms
long notes	short notes	different rhythmic groupings
anacrusis	paired quavers	semiquavers

CHORDS

To accompany your melody, you should also create a chord sequence. You will need to use appropriate chords, and make sure you know what notes are contained in each chord.

Consider the following questions:

1. What notes are in the chord of G?
2. What notes are in the chord of E minor?
3. What notes are in the chord of C?
4. What notes are in the chord of D?

See page 14 for a reminder if needed.

PLAN

Follow the plan below to compose your Scottish waltz.

1. **Section A**
   a) Compose an 8-bar melody using the notes of the pentatonic scale based on G.
   b) Create a chord sequence to accompany your melody using the chords **G, C** and **D**. You could try using the chord of **Em** (i.e. E minor) occasionally for a little bit of variety.
   c) Use the chord of **G** in bar 1.
   d) Experiment with the chords suggested above, trying to change to a new chord at the beginning of every bar.
   e) Explore other musical ideas by experimenting with some appropriate melodic and rhythmic concepts.
   f) Repeat your 8-bar melody and chord sequence. Try to develop this by varying your musical ideas to make it more interesting.

2. **Section B**
   a) Compose a contrasting 8-bar melody using the notes of the pentatonic scale based on G.
   b) Create a new chord sequence to accompany your melody using the chords **G, C, D** and **Em**. You could try using **Em** more to contrast with the first section.
   c) Again, explore some appropriate melodic and rhythmic features, but try to develop them to make this different from **Section A**.

3. **Section A(2)**

Repeat **Section A**. However, you should try to develop this by not repeating it exactly. Try to vary it slightly, for interest.

Finally, you could develop your waltz further by adding a bass line, an accompanying part or countermelody, four bars at the beginning, as an introduction, and four bars at the end as a **coda**.

contd

The music of Scotland – Composing a Scottish waltz

Here are some ideas you might use to develop your composition, using the first phrase of the Scottish tune *Ye Banks and Braes* as an example:

- Adding appropriate chords to accompany the melody.

- Developing this idea further by creating a broken chord accompaniment from the chords you have added.

- Making the texture more interesting by adding a simple bass part.

- Developing the texture further by creating an accompanying part or a **countermelody**, to be played by another instrument.

THINGS TO DO AND THINK ABOUT

Follow the plan above to compose your Scottish waltz.

Use the 'Composing a Scottish Waltz' templates (available at www.brightredbooks.net/N5Music) to help you to compose your waltz using music notation.

Consider which particular instruments, or sounds, will be most suitable for each of the parts.

DON'T FORGET

Your teacher will give you more advice about developing musical ideas in your waltz.

ONLINE

Check out the worksheet at www.brightredbooks.net/N5Music

DON'T FORGET

Write the time signature at the appropriate place at the beginning of the music, and make sure that your music notation is written clearly and is neatly spaced out.

ONLINE

Complete the composing review template at www.brightredbooks.net/N5Music

DON'T FORGET

Remember that a **waltz** has three beats in the bar, and many Scottish tunes use a **pentatonic scale**.

WORLD MUSIC

CARIBBEAN, INDIAN AND SOUTH AMERICAN MUSIC

WORLD MUSIC: INTRODUCTION

Different countries have their own individual musical styles and traditions. In many cases, it is the instruments that create the distinct sound associated with a particular style or country.

In this section you are going to find out about some musical styles and instruments associated with different countries.

The main styles that you will learn about are:

- **Latin American**
- **African**
- **Indian**

The main instruments and groups that you will learn about are:

- **Steel band** – from the Caribbean
- **Pan pipes** – from South America
- **Acoustic guitar** and **castanets** – from Spain
- **Guiro** and **bongo drums** – associated with **Latin American** music
- **Sitar** and **tabla** – associated with **Indian** music
- **Drums** and other **percussion instruments** – from **African** music.

CARIBBEAN MUSIC

Steel drums are found all over the world, but originate from Trinidad and Tobago in the Caribbean.

They were originally made from oil drums left on the Caribbean islands after the Second World War.

Steel drums are acoustic tuned percussion instruments that can play a variety of notes.

There are several different sizes of steel drum (or pan), each producing a different range of notes.

A **steel band** is a group of musicians who play music on steel drums (or pans).

A typical steel band will have a selection of steel drums, and possibly other instruments.

Steel band music is usually lively and energetic.

VIDEO LINK

Head to www.brightredbooks.net/N5Music for an example of steel drum playing.

VIDEO LINK

Listen to an example of a steel band playing at www.brightredbooks.net/N5Music

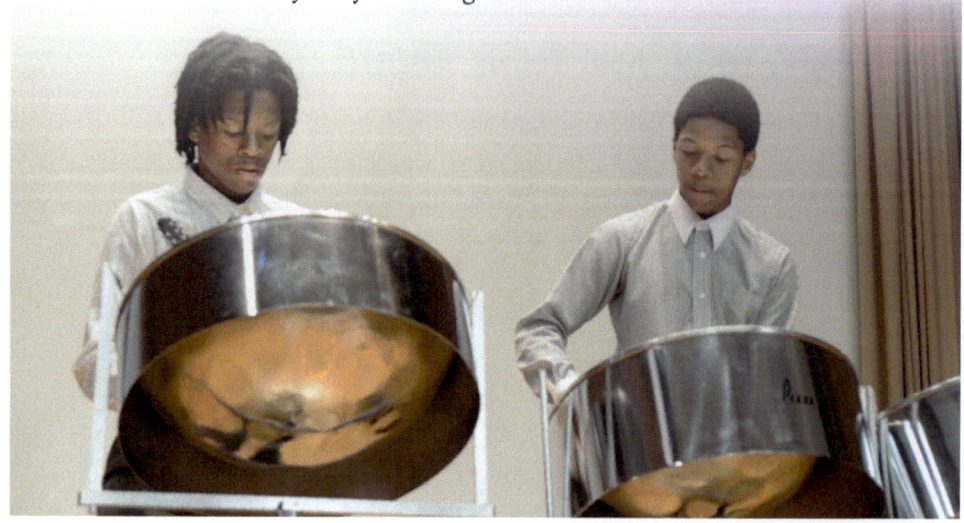

World music – Caribbean, Indian and South American music

INDIAN MUSIC

Indian music, like many other styles of traditional music, is not generally written down. Instead, musicians learn patterns of notes or scales called *raga*s and rhythms called *tala*s. The music is then improvised around these *raga*s and *tala*s. Popular instruments associated with Indian music are the **sitar** and **tabla**.

The sitar is a stringed instrument from northern India. As with a guitar, the performer can pluck the strings of the sitar with their fingers, or use a plectrum.

Melodies played on the sitar use special scales (combinations of notes) called *raga*s and rhythms called *tala*s.

The sitar is often accompanied by a small pair of small drums known as a tabla.

The larger drum is played by the left hand and produces the lower notes.

The smaller drum is played by the right hand and produces the higher notes.

VIDEO LINK
Listen to an example of a sitar playing at www.brightredbooks.net/N5Music

VIDEO LINK
Listen to an example of tabla playing at www.brightredbooks.net/N5Music

DON'T FORGET
The sitar and tabla are common instruments in Indian music.

VIDEO LINK
Listen to an example of pan pipes playing at www.brightredbooks.net/N5Music

SOUTH AMERICAN MUSIC

South American music comes from the area around the Andes, including countries such as Peru, Bolivia, Argentina, Venezuela and Chile. The traditional music of the Andes is called *Huayno* which is known for its use of **pan pipes**, or pan flutes.

Pan pipes are made from bamboo and are usually bound together in two or three rows. They come in different sizes, producing different ranges of notes.

The lower notes are produced by the longer pipes and higher notes produced by the shorter ones. The distinctive breathy sound is produced by blowing across the top of the pipes.

THINGS TO DO AND THINK ABOUT

1. Which two instruments are commonly associated with Indian music?
2. Which wind instrument from South America has a distinctive breathy tone?
3. What type of percussion group plays Caribbean music?

ONLINE TEST
Head to www.brightredbooks.net/N5Music to test yourself on Caribbean, Indian and South American music.

WORLD MUSIC

LATIN AMERICAN, SPANISH AND AFRICAN MUSIC

LATIN AMERICAN MUSIC

Latin American music is a lively style of dance music from countries like Brazil and Cuba.

Dances like the samba and salsa often feature **percussion** instruments such as conga drums, **bongo drums**, claves and the **guiro**.

Bongo drums originated in Cuba and are often used in Latin American music.

Bongo drums have fairly high pitches, are joined in pairs and are usually played with the fingers and palms of the players' hands. They are also sometimes played using drumsticks.

A **guiro** is made of wood that has been hollowed out and has ridges cut into the outer surface. A wooden stick is scraped along the ridges to produce the ratchet-like sound.

SPANISH MUSIC

Flamenco is a popular type of singing and dancing from Spain.

It includes:

- *Cante* – singing
- *Toque* – guitar playing
- *Baile* – dancing
- *Palmas* – handclaps.

The Spanish guitar is a type of **acoustic guitar** that uses nylon strings.

It is slightly smaller than a standard acoustic guitar, making it easier to hold.

Castanets are small hand-held percussion instruments that are very common in Spanish music.

They are made from wood and are held in the player's hands.

VIDEO LINK

Listen to examples of bongo drums at www.brightredbooks.net/N5Music

VIDEO LINK

Listen to examples of a guiro and Latin American music at www.brightredbooks.net/N5Music

DON'T FORGET

Latin American music often features lively dance styles such as samba and salsa.

VIDEO LINK

Listen to an example of Spanish guitar playing at www.brightredbooks.net/N5Music

VIDEO LINK

Listen to the example of Spanish guitar playing, accompanied by castanets at www.brightredbooks.net/N5Music

World music – Latin American, Spanish and African music

AFRICAN MUSIC

African music often features a variety of tuned and untuned percussion instruments, as well as singing and dancing. Percussion instruments commonly associated with African music include a wide range of drums, gongs and bells, as well as different kinds of xylophones.

African drums are often played in large groups. They come in all shapes and sizes and are usually made from hollowed logs and animal skins.

The 'talking drum' was originally used for communication between villages. Tightening the straps makes the pitch of the notes higher and loosening the straps makes the pitch of the notes lower.

The djembe, originally from West Africa, is a rope-tuned skin-covered drum played with the players' bare hands. This is a very popular instrument in an African drum ensemble.

VIDEO LINK

Listen to an example of the 'talking drum' at www.brightredbooks.net/N5Music

VIDEO LINK

Listen to an example of African drumming at www.brightredbooks.net/N5Music

ACTIVITY: Influences of world music on popular music

Explore the influence of world music styles on some styles of popular music.

For example, consider the influence of:

- Caribbean music on *Under The Sea* from *The Little Mermaid*
- African music on *The Lion Sleeps Tonight*
- African music on Paul Simon's *Graceland* album
- Indian music on *Within You, Without You* from The Beatles' *Sgt. Pepper's Lonely Hearts Club Band*
- Latin American music on *The Girl from Ipanema*.

DON'T FORGET

African music often features a variety of drums, percussion instruments and singing.

ONLINE

Head to www.brightredbooks.net/N5Music to hear the examples listed.

THINGS TO DO AND THINK ABOUT

Prepare a short presentation on an aspect of world music.

Choose a country that interests you and then:

1. Make a list of the musical instruments or styles from that country.
2. Identify appropriate melodic, harmonic and rhythmic concepts in the music.

Use audio or video clips to illustrate examples of the style.

ONLINE TEST

Head to www.brightredbooks.net/N5Music to test yourself on Latin American, Spanish and African music.

WORLD MUSIC

COMPOSING IN A LATIN AMERICAN OR CALYPSO STYLE

You are going to compose a melody in a **Latin American** or Calypso style making use of the chords C, F and G, as well as some syncopated rhythms.

Chord	Notes contained in the chord
C	C, E and G
F	F, A and C
G	G, B and D

HARMONY

You will use notes contained in the chords C, F and G. Make sure you know which notes are contained in each chord.

Here are the notes of these chords on the stave:

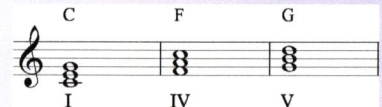

MELODY

Here are the notes of each of the above chords outlined as a simple melodic idea.

Play these notes on your chosen instrument to familiarise yourself with the pattern.

RHYTHM

Here are the same notes of each chord developed by using **syncopation** – a rhythmic feature in which the stress falls on a weak beat, or between beats, rather than on a strong beat.

Try playing these phrases so that you become familiar with the syncopated rhythms, as well as the notes of the chords.

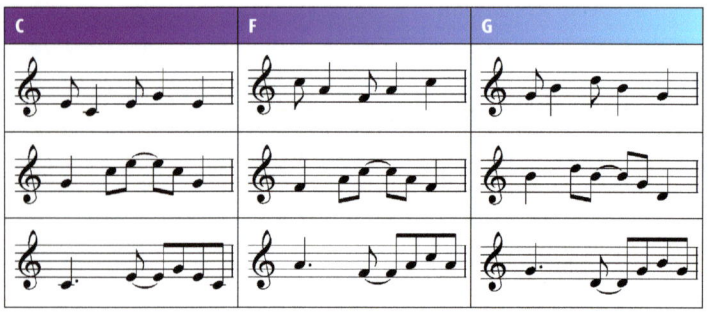

Here is a bank of melodic and rhythmic patterns that you could explore and experiment with. There are three examples for each chord.

Try playing these phrases so that you become familiar with the different syncopated rhythms, as well as the notes of the chords. Develop these ideas further by creating some other rhythms of your own.

COMPOSING A MELODY OVER A CHORD PROGRESSION

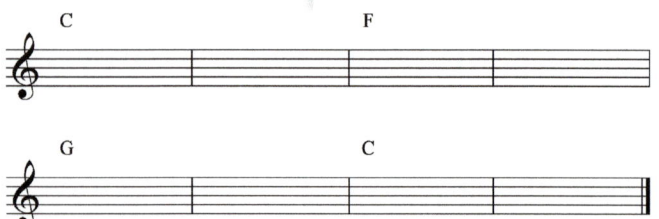

Now compose a melody of eight bars, in either a Latin American or Calypso style, over the given chord progression.

Start by choosing appropriate melodic and rhythmic phrases from the table above.

These phrases should include the appropriate notes from each chord along with a syncopated rhythm.

Although you should select an appropriate phrase for the corresponding chord, you may also consider using some passing notes (i.e. notes that come between the notes of the chord) to make your melody more interesting.

contd

World music – Composing in a Latin American or Calypso style

Try to use a variety of rhythms, including some syncopation. Although you can start with the melodic and rhythmic patterns above, you should also try to create some of your own.

If you are composing your piece of music on an electronic keyboard, or using a composing app, try experimenting with **Latin** rhythm styles such as Samba, Rumba, Cha-cha, Calypso or Bossa Nova to accompany your melody.

TIMBRE

Consider the instruments and sounds that you would like to use in your composition.

If you are composing using an electronic keyboard or composing app, try experimenting with some suitable instrumental sounds, tones or effects such as pan flute, reeds, brass, guitars, steel drums, percussion effects and drum fills.

STRUCTURE

Now that you have composed a basic eight-bar melody, you may wish to consider developing your composition by adding other sections and making the piece into a **ternary form (ABA or AABA)** structure. This would involve composing a contrasting middle section, as well as possibly adding an introduction and a **coda**.

Use the suggested plan, which includes an introduction and **coda**, to develop your composition: section **A**, section **B** (a contrast) followed by a repeat of section **A**.

Introduction	A short beginning (approximately 4 bars), to start the piece off and lead into the first main section. It might incorporate some elements of the melody, chords, or rhythm from later on in the composition.
Section A(1)	First main section, comprising the first statement of your: • melody • harmony/chord progression • bass line • simple accompaniment.
Section A(2)	This could be more or less a repeat of the first section, but with some possible developments that might include: • the melody being varied or altered in some way • the addition of a countermelody or other instrument parts • the chord progression being changed at the end to lead into the next section • the bass line being varied, or made more elaborate (possibly using passing notes) • the accompaniment being varied • instruments/sounds/tones being changed or varied.
Section B	This should be a contrasting section. Contrasts might include: • a new melody • a new chord progression • different chords being used (for example, Am) • a change to a new key (possibly from C major to A minor) • a different accompaniment • a different bass line.
Section A(3)	This could be more or less a repeat of the first **A** section, but with some possible further developments that might include: • the melody being further varied or altered in some way • the addition of another countermelody or other instrument parts • the chord progression being changed at the end to lead into a **coda** • the accompaniment being further varied, to add interest • the instruments/sounds/tones being changed or varied again.
Coda	A short concluding section (approximately 4 bars), to draw the piece to a convincing end. It might incorporate some elements from your section A melody or harmony.

DON'T FORGET

Write the time signature at the appropriate place at the beginning of the music, and make sure that your music notation is written clearly and is neatly spaced out.

DON'T FORGET

Try to develop your composition by experimenting with different concepts.

VIDEO LINK

Listen to some Caribbean and Calypso music for other ideas of what you might include in your composition at www.brightredbooks.net/N5Music

ONLINE TEST

Head to www.brightredbooks.net/N5Music to complete your composing review.

THINGS TO DO AND THINK ABOUT

Follow the plan above to compose a Latin American or Calypso style piece of music.

Add other accompanying parts such as harmony, broken chords, countermelody or bass.

Use the 'Composing in a Latin American or Calypso style' templates (available at www.brightredbooks.net/N5Music) to help you to compose your piece using music notation.

POPULAR MUSIC

BLUES, GOSPEL AND RAGTIME

The term 'popular music' refers to a number of styles and genres of music that have had popular appeal, or have been commercially successful. As musical styles constantly change and develop, our understanding of popular music also changes. Popular music encompasses a range of styles throughout the twentieth and twenty-first centuries and changes with each new generation.

Popular music styles from early in the twentieth century include styles such as **Blues, Gospel, Ragtime, Jazz** and **Swing.**

During the twentieth century, other styles such as **Rock'n'roll, Rock, Pop, Reggae, Rap** and **Celtic Rock**, as well as many other styles and sub-genres, also became popular.

BLUES

Blues is a style of music that originated in the late 1800s in the southern states of America. Blues developed from the spirituals and work-songs sung by African-American slaves, who would generally have worked in the cotton fields or vegetable plantations. With the end of slavery in 1865, the slaves experienced poverty and homelessness. They were often denied job opportunities and faced many other types of mistreatment.

The word 'blues' can also mean a feeling of sadness or melancholy. Many Blues songs tell of the troubles and hard lives led by the people.

Blues music often has 4 beats in a bar and is mostly patterned on a 12-bar structure (although 8 and 16 bars are also found). Blues melodies are often based on a Blues scale, which includes some altered notes.

> **VIDEO LINK**
>
> Listen to *Cross Road Blues*, a song by the influential Blues singer Robert Johnson, at www.brightredbooks.net/N5Music. This is a typical example of an early Blues song, accompanied by a guitar.

> **ACTIVITY**
>
> Explore some of the important influences on Blues by considering the following questions:
>
> - To what extent did the experience of slavery influence Blues music? Try to find some specific examples.
> - To what extent did Blues influence other styles of music? Try to identify some specific examples.

GOSPEL

Gospel music also developed in the late 1800s in the southern states of America. Like Blues, Gospel music was also originally performed by African-Americans and developed from spirituals and work-songs sung by slaves.

Gospel songs had religious words, and would often be sung in praise or thanksgiving to God. Gospel songs were generally very happy and joyful. People singing Gospel songs would often clap their hands or stamp their feet in time to the music.

> **VIDEO LINK**
>
> Listen to *Oh Happy Day* at www.brightredbooks.net/N5Music. This is a typical example of the Gospel style, featuring call and response – when the chorus (choir) in the background repeat the phrases sung by the soloist.

RAGTIME

Ragtime is another style of music that developed in the late 1800s. It was originally a style of piano playing that was popular in the saloons, bars and cafés of the Southern States of America. It became particularly popular in America and then in Europe in the early 1900s.

contd

Popular Music – Blues, Gospel and Ragtime

The most well-known composer of Ragtime was Scott Joplin, who composed over forty rags, marches and waltzes. One of his early pieces, *Maple Leaf Rag*, became so popular that it earned Scott Joplin the nickname 'the King of Ragtime'. With the increasing commercial success of other styles, such as Jazz and Swing, Ragtime fell from popularity around the 1920s. There was a huge revival of interest in Ragtime in the 1970s, however, mainly because one of Scott Joplin's rags, *The Entertainer*, was used as the theme music for the film *The Sting*.

Scott Joplin

Usually played on the piano, Ragtime features a melody (played by the right hand) making use of **syncopation**. This melody would be accompanied by a steady vamp-style bass (played by the left hand) which often incorporates wide leaps. Ragtime usually has 2 or 4 beats in a bar and is played at a steady tempo.

Pineapple Rag begins with a four-bar introduction played in **octaves** (i.e. the right and left hands are both playing the same notes but an octave apart). Many Ragtime piano pieces begin in this way.

Another typical example of Ragtime, *The Entertainer* begins with a four-bar introduction played in octaves on the piano.

VIDEO LINK

Listen to *Maple Leaf Rag* by Scott Joplin at www.brightredbooks.net/N5Music. This is a typical example of the Ragtime style and was one of Scott Joplin's most popular pieces.

VIDEO LINK

Listen to *Pineapple Rag* by Scott Joplin at www.brightredbooks.net/N5Music

VIDEO LINK

Listen to *The Entertainer* by Scott Joplin at www.brightredbooks.net/N5Music

DON'T FORGET

Syncopation is a rhythmic concept featuring strongly accented notes played on the weaker beats in a bar. Syncopation can be found in all kinds of music but is a common feature of Ragtime, Jazz, Swing and other styles of popular music.

ONLINE TEST

Test your knowledge of Blues, Gospel and Ragtime at www.brightredbooks.net/N5Music

THINGS TO DO AND THINK ABOUT

Ragtime pieces often use a set structure, based on four themes or melodies, each lasting about sixteen bars. We usually refer to these themes by letter names A, B, C and D. The themes are often played in the order A A B B A C C D D.

Listen to any of the Ragtime pieces listed above and try to identify where each of the different themes starts.

POPULAR MUSIC

JAZZ AND SWING

JAZZ

Jazz is a style of music that became popular in the early 1900s. However, like **Blues**, Jazz also had its roots in slavery. With the ending of slavery and the American Civil War, in 1865, there was not the same need for military bands. As the instruments were no longer needed, these second-hand instruments (including **clarinets**, **cornets** and **trombones**) were acquired by many of the newly-freed slaves, who would have been familiar with hymn tunes and European march tunes that had been played by military bands.

The earliest type of Jazz (sometimes known as Traditional Jazz or Dixieland Jazz) originated in New Orleans around the early 1900s, becoming very popular in the 1920s. This early form of Jazz was performed by a small group of musicians. The common instrumental line-up was clarinet, trumpet (or cornet) and trombone, which would have been the old military band instruments. The rhythm section generally featured a **double bass, piano** and **drum kit**.

An important feature of Jazz is the use of **improvisation**. This is when the performers make up their own version of the music during the performance. There may be a suggested chord sequence as a guide and the performers would create new melodies over the chords. Sometimes they might vary the original melody.

A Jazz band from New Orleans called 'The Original Dixieland Jazz Band' made the very first Jazz recording in 1917. The song was called *Livery Stable Blues*. This is a typical example of early Jazz, with the performers on the main melody instruments all improvising.

INSTRUMENTS OF JAZZ AND SWING

There are a number of instruments, and instrumental groups, that are commonly associated with Jazz and **Swing**. You have already learned about the combination of instruments featured in the earliest style of Jazz. In the National 5 Music question paper, you may be asked to identify either individual instruments or combinations of instruments.

VIDEO LINK

 Listen to *Livery Stable Blues* by The Original Dixieland Jazz Band at www.brightredbooks.net/N5Music

VIDEO LINK

Listen to an example of a clarinet playing New Orleans style Jazz at www.brightredbooks.net/N5Music

VIDEO LINK

 Listen to legendary Jazz musician Louis Armstrong playing the trumpet at www.brightredbooks.net/N5Music

VIDEO LINK

 Listen to an example of a trombone playing Jazz at www.brightredbooks.net/N5Music

VIDEO LINK

 Listen to an example of Jazz saxophone playing at www.brightredbooks.net/N5Music

ACTIVITY

Listen to examples of these individual instruments so that you are confident at recognising them.

1. Clarinet
2. Trumpet
3. Trombone
4. Saxophone
5. Double bass
6. A combination of piano, double bass and drum kit.

Jazz clarinettist Benny Goodman

Trombone player and bandleader Glenn Miller

Jazz trumpet player and singer Louis Armstrong

contd

Popular Music – Jazz and Swing

Walking bass

A **walking bass** is a bass line, usually played by the **double bass** or **bass guitar**, which moves mainly on every beat. A walking bass is a common feature of a variety of popular styles including Jazz and Swing.

Scat singing

Scat singing is a type of vocal improvisation found in Jazz, often making use of nonsense words and meaningless syllables such as 'do-be-do-wap' or 'bop-she-wha'. Sometimes the singer imitates the sounds of instruments.

Jazz vocalist Ella Fitzgerald

SWING

Swing is a style of dance music that became popular in the 1930s and 1940s. Swing is normally be played by larger groups of musicians called big bands or swing bands, featuring a wider range of instruments including saxophones, trumpets and trombones, as well as clarinets, piano, bass and drum kit. Swing music often features solo musicians who improvise over written arrangements of popular songs.

Swing gained widespread popularity mainly through developments in sound recording and radio broadcasting. Many of the bands playing Swing music had a bandleader. Some of the best-known bandleaders of the Swing style were Count Basie, Duke Ellington, Benny Goodman, Woody Herman and Glenn Miller.

THINGS TO DO AND THINK ABOUT

Make a list of the instruments commonly associated with Jazz and Swing.

Which concept is used to describe the vocal improvisation sometimes used in Jazz?

Which rhythmic concept is used to describe strongly accented notes played on the weaker beats of a bar?

VIDEO LINK

A popular combination of instruments playing Jazz is piano, double bass and drum kit. Listen to an example of this combination of instruments playing *C Jam Blues* at www.brightredbooks.net/N5Music

VIDEO LINK

Listen to an example of a walking bass at www.brightredbooks.net/N5Music

VIDEO LINK

Listen to the legendary Jazz vocalist Ella Fitzgerald scat singing at www.brightredbooks.net/N5Music

DON'T FORGET

A walking bass is a bass line that has one note on every beat, and is usually played by the double bass or bass guitar.

DON'T FORGET

Scat singing is type of vocal improvisation found in Jazz.

DON'T FORGET

Swing is a style of dance music featuring instruments such as saxophones, trumpets and trombones, as well as piano, double bass and drum kit.

ONLINE TEST

Test your knowledge of Jazz and Swing at www.brightredbooks.net/N5Music

VIDEO LINK

Listen to an example of the Glenn Miller Orchestra playing the Swing classic *In The Mood* at www.brightredbooks.net/N5Music

POPULAR MUSIC

ROCK'N'ROLL, ROCK, POP, REGGAE, CELTIC ROCK AND RAP

During the 1950s and 1960s, a number of different styles of popular music emerged. These included **Rock'n'roll, Rock, Pop** and **Reggae**. **Celtic Rock** and **Rap** both became popular in the 1970s and 1980s.

ROCK'N'ROLL

Elvis Presley

Rock'n'roll became popular in the 1950s with charismatic performers such as Elvis Presley, Chuck Berry and Little Richard. Rock'n'roll is a lively style of music that had its roots in a combination of African-American genres such as **Blues, Jazz, Gospel** and **Swing** and was particularly popular with teenagers at the time. Alongside the emergence of Rock'n'roll, dance crazes such as the jitterbug and jive also became popular.

The typical line-up of a Rock'n'roll band usually included one or two **electric guitars** (one lead guitar and one rhythm guitar), a **bass guitar** (or **double bass**), and **drum kit**. Many Rock'n'roll songs followed a 12-bar blues chord progression.

VIDEO LINK

Listen to Elvis Presley singing the Rock'n'roll classic *Hound Dog* at www.brightredbooks.net/N5Music

VIDEO LINK

Listen to Eric Clapton performing the Rock classic *Layla* at www.brightredbooks.net/N5Music

ROCK

The term **Rock** can be used to describe a number of popular musical styles since the 1960s. Rock music is generally loud, with a heavy driving beat. A typical Rock group tends to feature a range of amplified instruments such as electric guitars, bass guitar and **keyboards**, as well as drum kit and vocals.

VIDEO LINK

Listen to examples of Pop music at www.brightredbooks.net/N5Music

POP

The term **Pop** generally refers to music that is commercially successful and has been in the charts, either recently or in the past. Pop music tends to appeal to a wide range of listeners. Features of Pop music include relatively short songs composed in a simple form, often with a verse-chorus structure in which the verses and choruses are repeated. A song that has two or more verses, with the same music repeated for each verse, is said to be in **strophic form**. Many popular songs have a contrasting middle section. This contrasting section is often eight bars long and is called a **middle 8**. Pop music often has memorable or catchy melodies. A typical Pop group tends to feature vocals, electric guitars, drum kit and keyboards.

Successful Pop groups have included The Beatles, Abba, Take That, The Spice Girls, Little Mix and One Direction.

Famous Pop singers have included Michael Jackson, Ed Sheeran, Kylie Minogue and Adele.

Popular Music – Rock'n'roll, Rock, Pop, Reggae, Celtic Rock and Rap

REGGAE

Reggae music originated in Jamaica in the late 1960s. It developed in Jamaica from different types of Caribbean music including Calypso, Mento and Ska.

Reggae generally has a loud **bass** playing a **riff**, and a distinct rhythm featuring **accents** on the second and fourth beats of the bar. A riff is a repeated musical phrase, found in many styles of popular music.

One musician who is particularly associated with Reggae music is Bob Marley.

Bob Marley

RAPPING

Rapping, also known as MCing or emceeing, is a style of music in which the performer speaks the lyrics in rhyme, generally to a regular beat. The backing music for **Rap** is often created by using excerpts, called samples, from other songs. The lyrics are usually very rapid and often make use of colloquial or slang words. Rapping is regarded as a sub-genre of hip-hop music.

CELTIC ROCK

Celtic Rock first became popular in the 1970s and 1980s. This is a style of music that mixes elements of traditional music (such as the use of bagpipes and fiddles) with elements of **Rock** music (such as electric guitars, bass guitar and drum kit). More information about Celtic Rock can be found in the Scottish music section of this study guide.

ACTIVITY

Listen to *Ballavanich* by the group Wolfstone at www.brightredbooks.net/N5Music

This is a typical example of Celtic Rock.

As you listen to *Ballavanich* by Wolfstone, try to identify the features of the music that suggest Celtic Rock. You should consider the instruments being played as well as any other features of the style.

THINGS TO DO AND THINK ABOUT

Listen to any song from a style of your choice. Create a plan of the song, identifying the prominent sections of the song, such as introduction, verse, chorus, middle 8 and **coda**.

Within your plan, try to identify any other prominent features, such as the instruments being played or any other melodic, harmonic or rhythmic features.

VIDEO LINK

Listen to Bob Marley performing *One Love* at www.brightredbooks.net/N5Music. This is a typical example of Reggae, featuring a riff played on the bass guitar.

VIDEO LINK

Listen to some examples of Rap at www.brightredbooks.net/N5Music

DON'T FORGET

Rock'n'roll is a lively style of music that contains elements of Swing.

DON'T FORGET

Pop music has memorable or catchy melodies and often has a **verse-chorus** structure.

DON'T FORGET

Rock music is generally loud, with a heavy driving beat.

DON'T FORGET

Reggae is a relaxed style of music featuring accents on the second and fourth beats of the bar.

DON'T FORGET

Celtic Rock is a style of music that mixes elements of traditional music with elements of Rock music.

DON'T FORGET

Rap is a style of music in which the performer speaks the lyrics in rhyme, generally to a regular beat.

ONLINE TEST

Test yourself on popular music styles at www.brightredbooks.net

POPULAR MUSIC

COMPOSING POPULAR MUSIC 1

For your composing assignment, you might decide to compose a song in a popular style or create an improvisation as part of a composition in a Jazz or Blues style.

If you compose a piece in either a **Pop** or **Rock** style, you could experiment with writing a song using a **verse and chorus** structure. To expand the structure of your song you could add an introduction, **middle 8** and **coda**. You might develop the song further by adding a **descant, countermelody** or **backing vocals**.

If you decide to improvise music, you might like to create an **improvisation** within a composition in a **Jazz** or **Blues** style. This would involve composing a piece of music in a Jazz or Blues style and then improvising a melody over an appropriate chord progression.

ONLINE

You will need to learn to play the Blues scales on your chosen instrument. Different versions of Blues scales, for transposing instruments, as well as versions for guitar tablature, can be found at www.brightredbooks.net

IMPROVISING IN A BLUES STYLE

In this section, you are going to create an improvisation in a Blues style. You will improvise a melody over a Blues chord progression.

In order to do this, you will need to know the following:

- the chords used in a Blues chord progression
- the names of the notes in each of the chords
- the notes that can be used in a **walking bass** for each chord
- the notes of the Blues scale that goes with each chord.

You can create your improvisation on any instrument of your choice.

HARMONY

Many songs in Jazz, Blues, Swing and Rock'n'roll styles are based on the 12-bar Blues chord progression, which uses three chords.

Here are the three chords that would be used, in the key of C major:

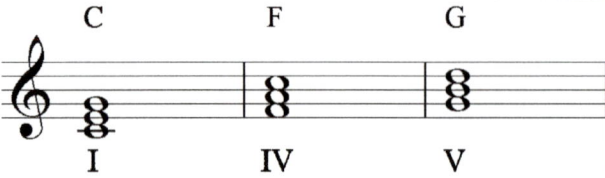

The following table lists the chord number, the chord name, and the three notes contained in each chord.

Chord number	Chord name	Notes contained in the chord
I	C	C, E and G
IV	F	F, A and C
V	G	G, B and D

contd

These three chords would then be played in the following order to create a 12-bar Blues chord progression:

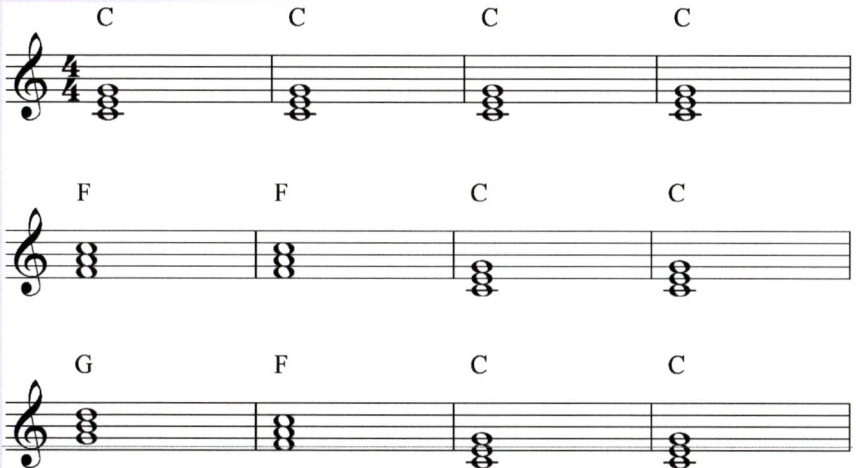

This progression can be repeated as many times as you want.

It is also common to have a walking bass playing in the background.

Here is a typical walking bass pattern that could be played along with the 12-bar Blues chord progression shown above:

DON'T FORGET

The 12-bar Blues chord progression is very common in a number of Blues, Swing and Rock'n'roll songs.

ONLINE TEST

Test yourself on popular music styles at www.brightredbooks.net/N5Music

THINGS TO DO AND THINK ABOUT

Try playing the 12-bar Blues chord progression on an instrument of your choice.

If you don't play a chordal instrument, you could try using the auto-chord facility of an electronic keyboard to allow you to play the chord progression using single notes.

Try playing the walking bass pattern on an instrument of your choice. It sounds particularly effective when played on a bass instrument, or on the low notes of a piano or keyboard.

If you play the 12-bar Blues chord progression on an electronic keyboard, using the auto-chord facility and a rhythm accompaniment style such as Big Band or Swing, the keyboard will generally play a walking bass pattern automatically.

POPULAR MUSIC

COMPOSING POPULAR MUSIC 2

MELODY

A common melodic feature of a lot of **Jazz** and **Blues** improvisations is the use of a **Blues scale**.

Blues scales generally have a number of accidentals (i.e. flats, sharps or naturals).

You will use Blues scales to improvise over the 12-bar Blues chord progression.

However, you will need to use the appropriate scale for each chord.

That means you will use the Blues scale based on C to improvise over the chord of C, the Blues scale based on F to improvise over the chord of F, and the Blues scale based on G to improvise over the chord of G.

Here are the three Blues scales that you will need to know to improvise over the 12-bar Blues chord progression on page 31.

Blues scale based on C:

Blues scale based on F:

Blues scale based on G:

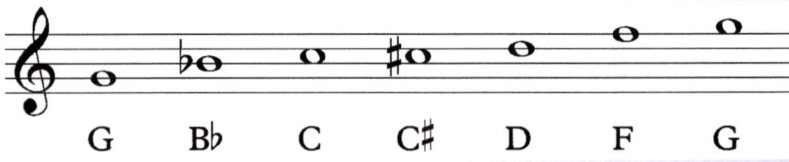

ONLINE

If you play a transposing instrument (such as the clarinet, trumpet or saxophone), or use guitar tablature, you will find a suitable version of the Blues scales at www.brightredbooks.net/N5Music

To become familiar with each Blues scale you should first practise them in smaller sections. For example, when starting to learn the Blues scale based on C, you should start by learning just the first four notes.

Here are the first four notes of the Blues scale on C:

The numbers printed above the notes are the finger numbers you should use if you are playing the notes on either the keyboard or piano. Start by playing up and down the four notes to become familiar with them. Then try to vary the order of the notes and improvise short phrases using only these four notes.

contd

Popular Music – Composing popular music 2

Once you are familiar with these four notes you should then do the same with the last three notes of the scale.

Here are the last three notes of the Blues scale based on C:

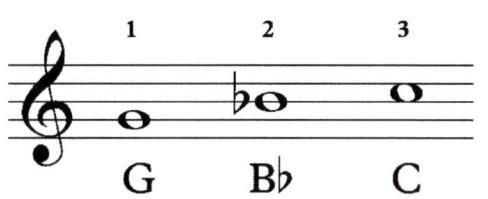

Again, the numbers printed above the notes are the finger numbers you should use if you are playing the notes on the keyboard or piano. You should start by playing up and down these three notes to become familiar with them, and then try to vary the order of the notes and improvise short phrases using only these three notes.

Once you are confident with improvising on each section of the Blues scale on C you should then try improvising using all the notes of the scale:

Once you are confident improvising with the full Blues scale on C, you should use the same process to learn the Blues scale on F and the Blues scale on G.

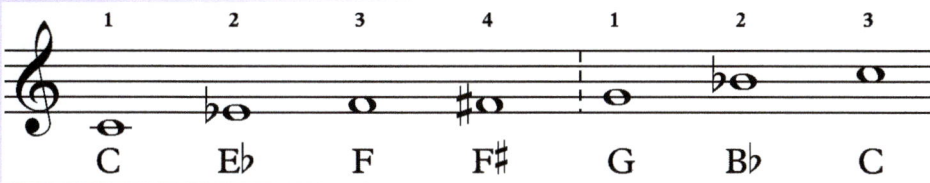

> **DON'T FORGET**
> Make sure that you are familiar with the appropriate Blues scale that goes with each chord.

> **DON'T FORGET**
> Although your composition may contain sections of improvisation, this must be in the context of a wider composition which demonstrates composing skills. A piece of music which is solely an improvisation is not acceptable.

ACTIVITY

Improvise a melody in a Blues style, over a 12-bar Blues chord progression.

Use the appropriate Blues scale for each chord.

If you play a melody instrument, you could ask someone else to play the chord progression or **walking bass** for you.

If you play the piano, you could try playing the walking bass with your left hand, while you improvise using the appropriate scales with your right hand.

If you play the electronic keyboard, or digital piano, you could use an appropriate rhythm accompaniment style such as Big Band or Swing as a backing for your improvisation.

Repeat the 12-bar Blues chord progression as many times as you like, trying to vary the improvisation each time.

As each chord in the chord progression changes, you should be prepared to improvise with the corresponding scale.

THINGS TO DO AND THINK ABOUT

To demonstrate that you have met the requirements of the composing assignment you should have evidence to show that you have:

- *Planned* your composition in a **Jazz** or **Blues** style.
- *Explored* and *experimented* with appropriate concepts such as a 12-bar Blues chord progression and the Blues scale.
- *Developed* musical ideas by adding a walking bass and some **improvisation**.
- *Reviewed* your own music, identifying what you like most about your composition, and what you could do to improve it.

VOCAL MUSIC

TYPES OF VOICES

VOCAL MUSIC: INTRODUCTION

Vocal music is any kind of music performed by one or more singers, with or without instrumental accompaniment. Vocal music can be found in a wide range of musical styles and genres. Singers who perform music in **Baroque, Classical** or **Romantic** styles, such as **opera**, often have the type of trained voices particularly suited to more 'classically' based styles. Singers who perform music in more popular styles, such as **Pop, Rock, Musicals**, or traditional music, often have voices suited more to these particular styles.

In this section, you will learn about different types of voices, as well as other styles and concepts associated with different aspects of vocal music.

TYPES OF VOICES

Female voices are generally divided into three main types: **soprano, mezzo-soprano,** and **alto** (also known as contralto).

Male voices are also generally divided into three main types: **tenor, baritone,** and **bass.**

These types of voice are, in the broadest sense, often defined by the range of notes that a singer can produce. However, we also need to consider the *tessitura*, which takes account of the overall range of notes contained in a song.

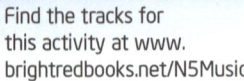

VIDEO LINK

Find the tracks for this activity at www.brightredbooks.net/N5Music

 **ACTIVITY**

Listen to a variety of different voices at www.brightredbooks.net/N5Music

For each voice the approximate range is shown.

A soprano is the highest type of female voice. Here is the approximate range of notes a soprano might be able to sing:

Listen to soprano Sarah Brightman singing *Wishing You Were Somehow Here Again* from the musical *Phantom of the Opera* by Andrew Lloyd Webber.

A mezzo-soprano is a mid-range female voice sitting between the higher soprano voice and the lower alto voice. Here is the approximate range of notes a mezzo-soprano might be able to sing:

Listen to mezzo-soprano Katherine Jenkins singing *Time To Say Goodbye*.

An alto (or contralto) is the lowest type of female voice. Here is the approximate range of notes an alto might be able to sing:

Listen to alto Janet Baker singing *Where Corals Lie* from *Sea Pictures* by Edward Elgar.

contd

Vocal Music – Types of voices

A tenor is the highest type of male voice. Here is the approximate range of notes a tenor might be able to sing:

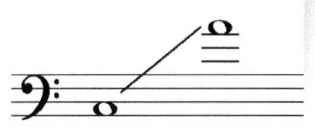

Listen to tenor Julian Ovenden singing *Younger Than Springtime* from the musical *South Pacific* by Rodgers and Hammerstein.

A baritone is a mid-range male voice sitting between the higher tenor voice and the lower bass voice. Here is the approximate range of notes a baritone might be able to sing:

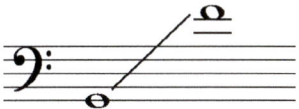

Listen to baritone Bryn Terfel singing the traditional American folksong *Shenandoah*.

A bass is the lowest type of male voice. Here is the approximate range of notes a bass might be able to sing:

Listen to bass Willard White singing *Ol' Man River* from the musical *Showboat* by Jerome Kern and Oscar Hammerstein II.

Voice	Description	Approximate vocal range
Soprano	Highest type of female voice.	
Mezzo-soprano	A mid-range female voice sitting between the higher soprano voice and the lower alto voice.	
Alto (or contralto)	Lowest type of female voice.	
Tenor	Highest type of male voice.	
Baritone	A mid-range male voice sitting between the higher tenor voice and the lower bass voice.	
Bass	Lowest type of male voice.	

DON'T FORGET

When identifying a type of voice, firstly try and decide if you are listening to a female or a male voice. Then try to decide if the overall *tessitura* of the voice is generally in the higher, medium or lower range. The table gives a brief description of each type of voice along with the approximate range of each voice.

ONLINE TEST

Test yourself on types of voice at www.brightredbooks.net/N5Music

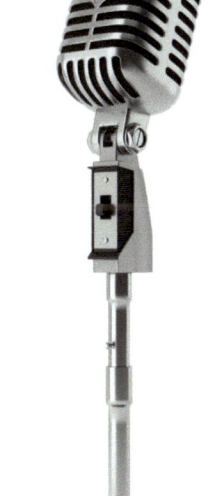

THINGS TO DO AND THINK ABOUT

Make sure that you are confident in being able to identify different types of voices.

VOCAL MUSIC

CHORAL MUSIC, MUSICALS AND OPERA

ONLINE TEST

Test yourself on types of voice at www.brightredbooks.net/N5Music

VIDEO LINK

Listen to *The Bluebird*, by the Irish composer Charles Villiers Stanford, for mixed choir, at www.brightredbooks.net/N5Music

MUSIC FOR CHOIR

A **choir** is a group of singers performing together. Choirs can be of any size, containing any combination of voices, and performing music in any style.

A female choir would usually consist of two groups of **sopranos** and one or two groups of **altos.**

A male choir may consist of any combination of **tenors, baritones,** and **basses,** although sometimes boys' voices (called trebles) can also be included.

The most common type of choir contains mixed voices (i.e. a mixture of male and female voices). The four main types of voice that form the basis of a standard mixed choir are soprano, alto, tenor and bass, often referred to by the initials **SATB** for short.

The Bluebird by Stanford (see video link) is a choral piece for sopranos, altos, tenors and basses, featuring a **solo** soprano voice.

It is also performed without any instrumental accompaniment. The concept used to describe any unaccompanied vocal performance is **a cappella**. This is an Italian term that literally means 'in the church style', and was originally applied to religious music sung in a church with no accompaniment. However, the term is now more generally used to describe any solo or group singing without instrumental accompaniment.

Also in this piece, notice that the choir of soprano, alto, tenor and bass voices are all singing the same rhythm, so the music sounds very chordal. The concept used to describe this type of chordal texture is **homophonic.** The solo soprano voice is singing a separate and more independent part from the rest of the choir. This is called a **countermelody.**

VIDEO LINK

You can hear examples of singing in unison, singing in harmony and a descant in the popular Christmas carol *O Come, All Ye Faithful* at www.brightredbooks.net/N5Music

UNISON, HARMONY AND DESCANT

If a group of singers are all singing the same notes at the same time, they are said to be singing in **unison**. If a mixed group of male and female singers sing the same notes at the same time it is likely that the female voices will be singing the notes an **octave** (i.e. eight notes) higher than the male voices. In this case we can refer to singing being in unison or octaves.

If a group of singers are singing two or more notes at the same time, to form **chords,** they are said to be singing in **harmony**.

A **descant** is a countermelody that is generally sung at a higher pitch than the main melody. Descants are commonly found in certain verses of hymn tunes and Christmas carols.

Examples of all these appear on the recording of *O Come, All Ye Faithful* (see video link). After an introduction, featuring brass instruments:

- Verse 1, beginning with the words 'O come, all ye faithful, Joyful and triumphant', features a choir singing in unison.
- Verse 2, beginning with the words 'God of God, Light of Light', features a choir singing in harmony.
- Verse 3, beginning with the words 'Sing, choirs of angels, Sing in exultation', features a descant sung by sopranos. Notice that the descant is sung at a higher pitch than the main melody.

DON'T FORGET

Singing in unison means a group of singers are all singing the same notes at the same time.

DON'T FORGET

Singing in harmony means a group of singers singing two or more notes at the same time.

DON'T FORGET

A cappella means singing without any instrumental accompaniment.

Vocal Music – Choral music, musicals and opera

MUSICAL

A **musical** is a theatrical stage production involving a combination of acting, spoken dialogue, singing and dancing. Musicals became popular during the twentieth century because they have appealing storylines, costumes and sets, as well as popular songs. Musicals usually consist of a number of solo songs, **duets** (songs for two people) and **chorus** numbers, and can be accompanied by an orchestra, band, or small instrumental ensemble. Within the context of a musical, the term chorus can be used to refer to either a group of singers or the music performed by a group of singers.

VIDEO LINK

Listen to *Memory* from the musical *Cats* at www.brightredbooks.net/N5Music. This is an example of a solo song from a musical.

VIDEO LINK

Listen to *Love is an Open Door* from the musical *Frozen* at www.brightredbooks.net. This is an example of a duet from a musical.

OPERA

An **opera**, like a musical, is a theatrical stage production involving a combination of acting, singing and dancing. In an opera, however, there is generally no spoken dialogue as everything is sung. It is thought that opera originated around the end of the sixteenth century in Florence, Italy. Operas have been written by many composers throughout the **Baroque**, **Classical** and **Romantic** periods, as well as during the twentieth and twenty-first centuries.

An opera features **arias** and **choruses** and is generally accompanied by an **orchestra**.

An **aria** is a **solo** song from an opera, accompanied by an orchestra. It would usually be in **strophic** form, meaning that the same music would be repeated for each verse.

A **chorus** is a song in an opera, or musical, featuring a group of singers. The term chorus can be used to refer to either a group of singers, or the music performed by a group of singers.

VIDEO LINK

Listen to *Do You Hear The People Sing?* from the musical *Les Misérables* at www.brightredbooks.net/N5Music. This is an example of a chorus from a musical.

DON'T FORGET

Whereas singers in musicals tend to have lighter and more natural-sounding voices, singers in operas tend to have more powerful voices.

VIDEO LINK

Listen to *La donna è mobile* from the opera *Rigoletto*, by Verdi, at www.brightredbooks.net/N5Music. This is an example of an aria from an opera, sung by a tenor. As the same music is repeated for each verse this aria is in strophic form.

VIDEO LINK

Listen to the *Pilgrims' Chorus* from the opera *Tannhäuser*, by Wagner, at www.brightredbooks.net/N5Music. This is an example of a chorus from an opera. The piece begins **a cappella** and with a **homophonic** texture. Later on there is a **crescendo** as the orchestra joins in.

THINGS TO DO AND THINK ABOUT

Make a list of the similarities and differences between musical and opera. Think about different styles of music, the kinds of voices that might be performing, and the type of accompaniment.

VOCAL MUSIC

WORD SETTING, SONG STRUCTURE AND BACKING VOCALS

VIDEO LINK

Listen to *Make You Feel My Love* performed by Adele at www.brightredbooks.net/N5Music

VIDEO LINK

Listen to *Ding Dong! Merrily on High* performed by the choir of King's College Cambridge at www.brightredbooks.net/N5Music

DON'T FORGET

Syllabic word setting is when each syllable is sung to one note only.

DON'T FORGET

Melismatic word setting is when several notes are sung to one syllable.

VIDEO LINK

Listen to *Caledonia* performed by Dougie MacLean at www.brightredbooks.net/N5Music

VIDEO LINK

Listen to *You Raise Me Up* performed by Westlife at www.brightredbooks.net/N5Music

VIDEO LINK

Listen to *I Can't Help Falling In Love With You* performed by Michael Bublé at www.brightredbooks.net/N5Music

SYLLABIC AND MELISMATIC WORD SETTING

When words are set to music, in a song or a choral piece, you will sometimes find that each syllable of a word is given a different note. This is known as **syllabic** word setting. However, words can also be set to music in such a way that several notes may be sung to one syllable. This is known as **melismatic** word setting. You should be able to tell the difference between syllabic and melismatic word setting by listening to a vocal performance.

Consider the song *Make You Feel My Love*, performed by Adele. Each syllable of every word is sung to a separate note. This is an example of syllabic word setting.

In the popular Christmas song *Ding Dong! Merrily on High*, the beginning of each verse features syllabic word setting. However, the word *Gloria* is sung over many notes. This is an example of melismatic word setting.

SONG STRUCTURES

A song that has two or more verses, with the same music repeated for each verse, is said to be in **strophic** form. The words for each verse would generally be different, although the melody would be the same.

Many popular songs also use a **verse and chorus** structure. This means that as well as having the same music repeated for each verse, there is a different section called a **chorus**. The chorus has different music to the **verses** and generally comes in between the verses. A chorus, as well as having the same music each time it is repeated, also has the same words.

Caledonia is a popular song that has the same music repeated for each verse. This means the song is in strophic form. However, it also makes use of a verse and chorus structure. The repeated section of the song that starts with the words 'Let me tell you that I love you' has the same words and music each time. This is called the chorus.

Another popular song that makes use of a verse and chorus structure is You Raise Me Up. The first verse is sung by a solo voice. This leads into the first chorus, starting with the words 'You raise me up'. The second verse is played as an instrumental, with no singing. Notice that this instrumental verse is being played in a higher key. This is known as a **change of key** or a **modulation**. This instrumental verse leads into the second chorus, starting again with the words 'You raise me up'. The chorus is then repeated once again. Notice that this third version of the chorus features another change of key, or modulation.

Many popular songs, whether or not they are based on a **verse and chorus** structure, have a contrasting middle section. This contrasting section is often eight bars long and is called a **middle 8**.

I Can't Help Falling In Love With You is another popular song that is in strophic form. However, it has a contrasting section in the middle of the song that starts with the words 'Like a river flows'. This section is called the middle 8.

Vocal Music – Word setting, song structure and backing vocals

BACKING VOCALS

Many popular songs, as well as featuring a lead singer or solo singer, will feature **backing vocals**. This is when other singers, or other members of the group, provide vocal harmonies in the background.

In *You're Gonna Lose That Girl,* by The Beatles, as well as the lead singer singing the main part of the song, listen out for the rest of the group providing backing vocals and accompanying harmonies in the background.

VIDEO LINK
Listen to *You're Gonna Lose That Girl,* performed by The Beatles, at www.brightredbooks.net/N5Music

DON'T FORGET
There are also a number of vocal styles associated with Scottish music, such as **mouth music, Scots ballads, bothy ballads, waulking songs** and **Gaelic psalms**. Examples of these can be found in the section on Scottish music. Also, vocal concepts such as **scat singing** and **rapping** can be found in the section on popular music styles.

ONLINE TEST
Test yourself on types of voice at www.brightredbooks.net

THINGS TO DO AND THINK ABOUT

Listen to some songs and analyse them by considering the following questions:

What is the structure of the song? Does it use a verse and chorus structure? Does it have an introduction, **coda** or a middle 8?

Is the word setting syllabic or melismatic?

Are there any other features, such as backing vocals or modulation?

TIMBRE – INSTRUMENTS AND HOW THEY ARE PLAYED

INSTRUMENTS OF THE ORCHESTRA: WOODWIND

In this section you will learn about how different instruments sound, and also about the way that sound is produced on different instruments. You will learn about the four main sections of the orchestra, followed by keyboard instruments and guitars.

THE FOUR SECTIONS OF THE ORCHESTRA

An **orchestra** is a large group of instruments made up of four main sections, or families, of instruments: **Woodwind, Brass, Strings** and **Percussion**. Most orchestras generally have a conductor who stands at the front, interpreting the music and keeping all the musicians playing in time. Orchestras play music in a variety of styles.

There are a variety of techniques available to musicians to produce sounds on different instruments. The most common include **striking (hitting), blowing, bowing (arco), plucking (pizzicato)** and **strumming**. You will also find out about other playing techniques, such as **flutter tonguing** and **con sordino**.

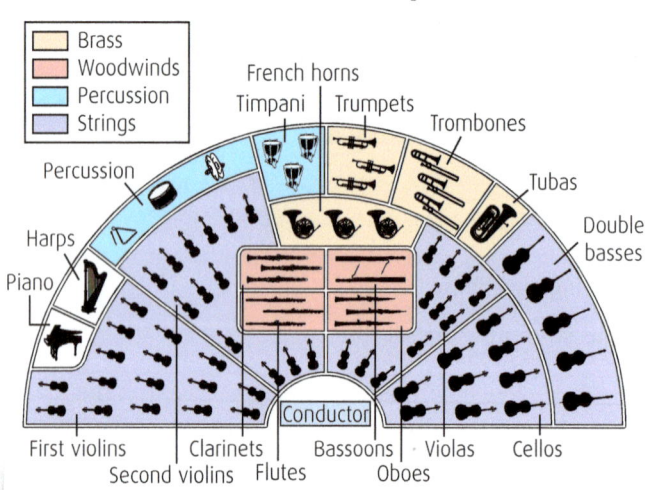

INSTRUMENTS OF THE ORCHESTRA: WOODWIND

Most orchestras feature four woodwind instruments: **flute, oboe, clarinet** and **bassoon**. The sound is produced on woodwind instruments by the player **blowing** into, or across, the mouthpiece, or into the reed, of the instrument, causing a column of air to vibrate. This method of producing sound is used with **woodwind** and **brass** instruments.

Flute

The flute is made from metal nowadays, although it was originally made from wood. The flute sounds bright and shrill, and generally plays the highest notes in the woodwind section. In an orchestra there are usually two flutes. In many orchestras there will also be a **piccolo**, which is a very small flute and can play extremely high notes. The piccolo is like a small flute that plays an octave (eight notes) higher than the flute. The piccolo is the smallest member of the woodwind family and, therefore, can play the highest range of notes.

> **VIDEO LINK**
> Listen to *Syrinx*, by Debussy, for solo flute, at www.brightredbooks.net/N5Music

> **VIDEO LINK**
> Listen to *Tweet*, by Daniel Dorff, for solo piccolo, at www.brightredbooks.net/N5Music

contd

Timbre – instruments and how they are played – Instruments of the orchestra: woodwind

Flutter tonguing is a playing technique in which the player rolls the letter 'r' while blowing into the instrument. It is used by wind players and is particularly effective for flute and brass.

Oboe

The **oboe** is made from wood and has metal keys. To make a sound, the player must blow into the double reed (two pieces of cane which vibrate together) to create the sound. There are usually two oboes in an orchestra, but in some larger orchestras there may also be a **cor anglais**, which is a larger version of the oboe. Because of the double reed, the oboe tends to have a distinct penetrating tone, and it is often used to create a melancholic mood.

Clarinet

The **clarinet** is also made from wood. It looks similar to an oboe but is slightly larger and does not use a double reed. Instead, the clarinet uses a single reed, which is attached to the mouthpiece (the part which the player blows into) with a metal band called a ligature. The clarinet can play a wide range of notes and produces a mellow sound. There are usually two clarinets in an orchestra, but in larger orchestras you may also find a **bass clarinet** (which can play lower notes).

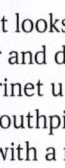

Bassoon

The **bassoon** is the largest and lowest-pitched of the standard woodwind instruments. It is too large for the player to blow in one end and be able to reach the keys so, there is a *crook*, which is a curved piece of metal tubing onto which the reed is placed. Like the oboe, the bassoon also uses a *double reed*. The bassoon can play the lowest notes of the woodwind section. There are usually two bassoons in an orchestra, but sometimes larger orchestras also feature a contrabassoon, which is much larger than a bassoon and can play extremely low notes.

VIDEO LINK

Listen to an example of flutter tonguing at www.brightredbooks.net/N5Music

VIDEO LINK

Listen to *Gabriel's Oboe* by Ennio Morricone at www.brightredbooks.net/N5Music

VIDEO LINK

Listen to *The Victorian Kitchen Garden* by Paul Reade, featuring a solo clarinet, at www.brightredbooks.net/N5Music

VIDEO LINK

Listen to part of *Scheherezade* by Rimsky-Korsakov, featuring a solo bassoon, at www.brightredbooks.net/N5Music

DON'T FORGET

Flutter tonguing is a method of producing sound in which the player rolls the letter 'r' while blowing into the instrument. It is commonly used on the flute.

THINGS TO DO AND THINK ABOUT

Listen to examples of woodwind instruments and make sure that you are able to tell one instrument from the other.

ONLINE TEST

Test your knowledge of woodwind instruments at www.brightredbooks.net/N5Music

TIMBRE – INSTRUMENTS AND HOW THEY ARE PLAYED

INSTRUMENTS OF THE ORCHESTRA: BRASS

The **brass** section consists of four instruments all made of metal: **trumpet, French horn, trombone** and **tuba**. All brass instruments consist of a mouthpiece (that the player blows into), a column of air that vibrates to produce the sound, and a bell (where the sound comes out).

VIDEO LINK
Listen to the *Fanfare for St. Edmundsbury* by Benjamin Britten, for three trumpets, at www.brightredbooks.net/N5Music

TRUMPET

The trumpet is the smallest and highest instrument in the brass section. Air vibrates through a player's lips and into a mouthpiece. The player then uses the three valves to change the pitch of the notes. The trumpet can play very loud and high.

VIDEO LINK
Listen to part of *Symphony No. 5* by Tchaikovsky, featuring a French horn solo, at www.brightredbooks.net/N5Music

FRENCH HORN

The **French horn** is made in a similar way to the trumpet but is a little larger. The player holds it by placing their right hand into the bell of the instrument while their left hand operates the three valves to change the pitch of the notes. The French horn produces a mellow sound.

VIDEO LINK
Listen to *Fantasy for Trombone* by Malcolm Arnold at www.brightredbooks.net/N5Music

TROMBONE

The **trombone** can be one of the loudest instruments in the orchestra. Unlike the trumpet and French horn, it does not have valves, but uses **a movable slide to** produce different notes. The trombone can play quite low notes.

VIDEO LINK
Listen to an example of a glissando being played on a trombone at www.brightredbooks.net/N5Music

The fact that the trombone uses **a movable slide to** change the pitch of the notes **means that it can** produce a characteristic effect of sliding from one note to another. The concept used to describe this sliding effect is **glissando**.

TUBA

The **tuba** is the largest of the brass instruments and has a very low range of notes. It also has valves which are used to change the pitch of the notes. Due to its size, the tuba is usually played with the player sitting down and resting the instrument on their knees.

VIDEO LINK

Listen to *Tuba Smarties* by Herbie Flowers at www.brightredbooks.net/N5Music

VIDEO LINK

Listen to a muted trumpet at www.brightredbooks.net/N5Music

CON SORDINO

Con sordino is an Italian term asking for a musician to use a mute.

This term is generally applied to brass and **string** instruments.

Brass players use a cone-shaped device called a mute, which is inserted into the bell of the instrument. This changes the tone of the instrument and reduces the volume.

VIDEO LINK

Listen to a wind band playing at www.brightredbooks.net/N5Music

VIDEO LINK

Listen to a brass band playing at www.brightredbooks.net/N5Music

DON'T FORGET

Con sordino is an Italian term for an instrument being muted.

WIND BAND AND BRASS BAND

A **wind band** is a group of musicians playing a variety of **woodwind**, **brass** and **percussion** instruments.

A **brass band** is a group of musicians playing a variety of brass and percussion instruments. Whereas the brass section of the orchestra features the trumpet, French horn, trombone and tuba, a brass band features instruments such as the **cornet** (like a trumpet), **flugelhorn**, **tenor horn** and **baritone horn**.

DON'T FORGET

Glissando is a sliding effect, often played on a trombone.

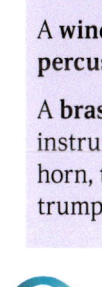

THINGS TO DO AND THINK ABOUT

Listen to examples of brass instruments and make sure that you are able to tell one instrument from the other.

Name some of the different brass instruments that you would expect to find in either a brass band or an orchestra.

ONLINE TEST

Test your knowledge of brass instruments at www.brightredbooks.net/N5Music

TIMBRE – INSTRUMENTS AND HOW THEY ARE PLAYED

INSTRUMENTS OF THE ORCHESTRA: STRINGS

The **string** section features four main instruments: **violin, viola, cello** and **double bass**. Sometimes the orchestra will also have a **harp**. The sound is produced on the four main stringed instruments by either by **bowing** or **plucking**.

BOWING AND PLUCKING

Bowing involves drawing a bow over the strings to make the strings vibrate. The bow is a long wooden stick with horsehairs stretched tightly from one end to the other. The Italian term used to describe this method of producing sound is **arco**.

Plucking involves the player using their fingers to pluck the strings. The Italian term used to describe this method of producing sound is **pizzicato** (sometimes abbreviated to **pizz.**).

VIDEO LINK

Listen to *Adagio for Strings* by Samuel Barber at www.brightredbooks.net/N5Music. This features a string orchestra playing arco.

VIDEO LINK

Listen to *Pizzicato Polka* by Johann Strauss at www.brightredbooks.net/N5Music. This features a string orchestra playing pizzicato.

Nicola Benedetti

VIOLIN

The violin is the smallest of the string instruments, so it can play the highest notes. It is made from wood and has four strings.

String instruments, like brass instruments, can be **muted**. The Italian term for this is **con sordino**. This involves placing a comb-shaped device over the strings to alter the tone.

VIDEO LINK

Listen to Nicola Benedetti playing *Méditation* from the opera *Thaïs* by Jules Massenet at www.brightredbooks.net/N5Music

VIDEO LINK
Listen to *Death of Åse* from *Peer Gynt Suite No. 1* by Edvard Grieg, featuring strings playing con sordino, at www.brightredbooks.net/N5Music

Timbre – instruments and how they are played – Instruments of the orchestra: strings

VIOLA

The **viola** is similar to the violin, but is a little larger so it can play slightly lower notes. It is played in the same way as the violin.

The viola has a rich and warm tone.

 VIDEO LINK

Listen to *Elegy* for solo viola by Stravinsky at www.brightredbooks.net/N5Music.

CELLO

The **cello** (short for violoncello) is larger than the viola and has a metal spike at the bottom. The cellist plays the cello while sitting down, with the metal spike on the ground, and rests the cello between their knees. The cello has a low and rich sound.

 VIDEO LINK

Listen to *The Swan* from *The Carnival of the Animals* by Camille Saint-Saëns at www.brightredbooks.net/N5Music.

DOUBLE BASS

The **double bass** is the largest of the string instruments. It stands on the floor and the player either stands or sits on a high stool to play it. The double bass often appears in Jazz bands as well as in the orchestra. It can be played with the bow but is often played pizzicato (i.e. plucked). The double bass can play notes which are lower than any of the other string instruments.

 VIDEO LINK

Listen to *The Elephant* from *The Carnival of the Animals* by Camille Saint-Saëns at www.brightredbooks.net/N5Music.

 VIDEO LINK

Listen to the harp solo in *Introduction and Allegro* by Ravel at www.brightredbooks.net/N5Music

HARP

The **harp** usually appears in large orchestras. The harp is made from a large wooden frame and is often decorated with carvings. It has around 47 strings and 7 pedals which change the pitch of certain notes. This helps the harp player to change key quickly. It is played by plucking the strings.

DON'T FORGET

Pizzicato is an Italian term for a string player to pluck the strings with their fingers.

DON'T FORGET

Arco is an Italian for a string player to use a bow to play the instrument.

THINGS TO DO AND THINK ABOUT

Listen to examples of string instruments and make sure that you are able to tell one instrument from the other.

Make a list of the four main string instruments in the orchestra in order of pitch, starting with the highest.

ONLINE TEST

Test your knowledge of string instruments at www.brightredbooks.net/N5Music

TIMBRE – INSTRUMENTS AND HOW THEY ARE PLAYED

INSTRUMENTS OF THE ORCHESTRA: PERCUSSION

The **percussion** section features a huge range of instruments such as **timpani, xylophone, glockenspiel, snare drum, tambourine, guiro, triangle** and many more. The number of percussion players in an orchestra will depend on the requirements of the music. The percussion section is usually situated at the back of the orchestra.

VIDEO LINK
Listen to a percussion ensemble at www.brightredbooks.net/N5Music. You will hear a number of different percussion instruments being played in a variety of ways; using sticks, beaters, and even the players' hands.

PLAYING TECHNIQUES

Sound can be produced on percussion instruments in a variety of ways, from being struck with beaters, sticks or mallets to being shaken or hit together. Sometimes the performer will use their own hands.

Percussion instruments can be divided into two main groups: **tuned percussion** and **untuned percussion**.

TUNED PERCUSSION

Tuned percussion instruments can play notes of different pitches. Some of them can play full melodies. The most common are the xylophone and the glockenspiel.

Xylophone

The xylophone is made from wood, and the wooden bars are set up in a similar way to notes on a keyboard.

VIDEO LINK
Listen to a xylophone solo at www.brightredbooks.net/N5Music

Glockenspiel

The glockenspiel is smaller than the xylophone and its bars are made from metal. It produces a very high and bright sound.

VIDEO LINK
Listen to a glockenspiel solo at www.brightredbooks.net/N5Music

Timpani

The timpani (or kettledrums) are tuned to different notes. The pitch of each drum is adjusted by a pedal which tightens or loosens the skin of the drum.

VIDEO LINK
Listen to a timpani solo at www.brightredbooks.net/N5Music

Rolls

Music played by percussion instruments often features **rolls**. A roll is a very fast repetition of a note on a percussion instrument, usually with alternating beaters or sticks.

VIDEO LINK
Listen to an example of a timpani roll at www.brightredbooks.net/N5Music

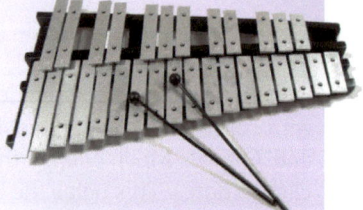

UNTUNED PERCUSSION

Untuned percussion instruments don't play specific notes or different pitches. Instead, they are used to add colour and atmosphere to the music.

Some of the most popular untuned percussion instruments are: **drum kit, snare drum, bass drum, cymbals, triangle, tambourine, guiro, castanets, hi-hat,** and **bongo drums**.

VIDEO LINK
Listen to a drum kit at www.brightredbooks.net/N5Music

contd

Timbre – instruments and how they are played – Instruments of the orchestra: percussion

Drum kit

A drum kit is a set of drums featuring a bass drum, floor toms, hi-hat, snare drum and cymbals.

1. Bass drum
2. Snare drum
3. Floor tom
4. Mid tom
5. High tom
6. Hi-hat
7. Ride cymbal
8. Crash cymbal

Snare drum

The **snare drum** (or side drum) has two drumheads stretched tightly over a hollow metal frame. The top head is struck with wooden drumsticks, and is called the batter-head. The bottom head, or snare-head, has metal wires called snares stretched tightly across it.

The snares produce a characteristic rattling sound as they vibrate against the bottom head.

Tambourine

The **tambourine** has a frame, often of wood or plastic, with pairs of small metal jingles, called 'zils'. Tambourines come in a variety of shapes with the most common being circular. The tambourine can be shaken or struck by the player's hands.

VIDEO LINK

Listen to a snare drum, a tambourine, a guiro, bongo drums, castanets and a triangle at www.brightredbooks.net/N5Music

Guiro

The **guiro** is a popular Latin American percussion instrument consisting of an open-ended, hollow wooden tube with parallel notches cut in one side. It's played by rubbing a stick along the notches to produce a ratchet-like sound.

Bongo drums

Bongo drums are high-pitched drums, joined in pairs and usually played by the palms of the performer's hands.

Castanets

Castanets are small hand-held percussion instruments popular in Spanish Flamenco music. The produce a very distinct clicking sound.

Triangle

The **triangle** is a percussion instrument which is a piece of metal in the shape of a triangle, open at one corner, and struck with a metal beater. It is an untuned percussion instrument, as it cannot play a range of notes.

DON'T FORGET

The bars of the glockenspiel are made from metal.

DON'T FORGET

The bars of the xylophone are made from wood.

ONLINE TEST

Test your knowledge of percussion instruments at www.brightredbooks.net/N5Music

THINGS TO DO AND THINK ABOUT

Listen to examples of percussion instruments and make sure that you are able to tell one instrument from the other.

Make a list of some un-tuned percussion instruments.

TIMBRE – INSTRUMENTS AND HOW THEY ARE PLAYED

KEYBOARDS AND GUITARS

KEYBOARD INSTRUMENTS

Keyboard instruments (such as the **piano**, **organ** and **harpsichord**) are played in a very similar way, by pressing down keys. However, the instruments all sound different because the actual sounds are produced in different ways.

Piano

The piano is a keyboard instrument which produces sounds by hammers striking strings. The piano can play a wide variety of **dynamics**, depending on how hard the keys are struck. Most have 88 keys, most of which are white, with the flats and sharps being black.

Harpsichord

The **harpsichord** is a keyboard instrument which looks like a small grand piano. The keys are laid out in the same way as on a piano but the colours are often the opposite way round. The harpsichord produces a distinctive sound that is produced by strings being plucked by quills when the keys are pressed. Harpsichords usually have two manuals (or keyboards), enabling the performer to play with some dynamic contrast. This is because each manual is able to play at a different volume level. However, it is not possible to play a crescendo or diminuendo on the harpsichord. The harpsichord is a common instrument in **Baroque** music. It was a popular keyboard instrument before the piano was invented.

Organ

The **organ** (or pipe organ) is a keyboard instrument that is often found in churches or cathedrals. It usually has two or more manuals (keyboards) and a pedal board. The organist plays the manuals (or keyboards) with their hands, while playing the notes on the pedal board with their feet.

In traditional pipe organs, the sound is produced by air being pushed through a series of pipes. However, nowadays it is quite common for smaller churches to have digital organs, where the sound is produced electronically.

A grand piano

VIDEO LINK

Listen to the **piano** at www.brightredbooks.net/N5Music

VIDEO LINK

Listen to the **harpsichord** at www.brightredbooks.net/N5Music

VIDEO LINK

Listen to the **organ** at www.brightredbooks.net/N5Music

DON'T FORGET

The harpsichord is a popular keyboard instrument in Baroque music.

GUITARS

Guitars come in all shapes and sizes and play different styles of music.

The most common types of guitars are **acoustic guitar**, **electric guitar** and **bass guitar**.

There are a variety of techniques that guitar players use to produce sound on their instruments. These include **strumming** and **plucking**, as well as effects such as **reverb** and **distortion**.

Acoustic guitar

An acoustic guitar is a guitar which does not require an electric amplifier to produce sound. It generally has six strings and is usually played by the performer either **plucking** or **strumming** the strings with their fingers, or using a plectrum.

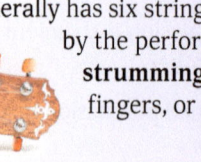

Timbre – instruments and how they are played – Keyboards and guitars

Strumming is a technique used by guitar players drawing their fingers, or a plectrum, across the strings.

Electric guitar

An electric guitar is a type of guitar that requires an electric amplifier to produce sound. Like an acoustic guitar, an electric guitar usually has six strings. An electric guitar, however, can produce a variety of different effects.

Electric guitars are often found playing **Pop** or **Rock** music.

A common musical feature of Pop and Rock styles is the use of a **riff.**

A riff is a repeated phrase commonly found in in a variety of popular music styles.

Bass guitar

A bass guitar generally has four strings and plays notes of a much lower pitch than the other guitars. Like the electric guitar, the bass guitar is amplified.

Reverb is an electronic effect which can give the impression of different acoustics, e.g. as if the performance has been recorded in a large hall, or even a cathedral.

Distortion is an electronic effect used in rock music to colour the sound of an electric guitar. It creates a 'fuzzy' sound rather than the usual clean sound.

 VIDEO LINK

Listen to *Stairway to Heaven* played on an acoustic guitar at www.brightredbooks.net/N5Music. This features plucking and **finger-picking**.

 VIDEO LINK

Listen to guitar strumming at www.brightredbooks.net/N5Music

 VIDEO LINK

Listen to an electric guitar playing a variety of riffs at www.brightredbooks.net/N5Music

 VIDEO LINK

Listen to **bass guitar** solos at www.brightredbooks.net/N5Music

 VIDEO LINK

Listen to an example of reverb at www.brightredbooks.net/N5Music

 VIDEO LINK

Listen to an example of distortion at www.brightredbooks.net/N5Music

 DON'T FORGET

An acoustic guitar does not require an amplifier to produce sound.

 DON'T FORGET

An electric guitar does require an amplifier to produce sound.

 ONLINE TEST

Test your knowledge of keyboard instruments and guitars at www.brightredbooks.net/N5Music

THINGS TO DO AND THINK ABOUT

Listen to examples of keyboard instruments and make sure that you are able to tell the difference between a piano, a harpsichord and an organ.

Listen to examples of different guitars and make sure that you can tell the difference between an acoustic guitar, an electric guitar and a bass guitar.

FORMS, STYLES AND PERIODS

MUSICAL FORMS

The musical forms that you will need to be able to recognise are:

- binary
- ternary
- rondo
- theme and variations.

BINARY FORM (AB)

A piece of music in **binary form** divides into *two* clear sections. We generally refer to these sections as section **A** and section **B**. Each section is often repeated.

ONLINE

Head to www.brightredbooks.net/N5Music for an activity on musical forms.

 ACTIVITY

1. Listen to the *Sarabande* by Corelli, for violin and harpsichord, while following the printed melody below. The music is in binary form so it has two clear sections (A and B).

Notice each section is repeated, and the violin decorates the melody during the repeat.

VIDEO LINK

Head to www.brightredbooks.net/N5Music to listen to the tracks for the activities in this section.

2. Listen to this excerpt again, while following the music above, and answer the following questions:
   - Is the tonality of the music **major** or **minor**?
   - Each section ends with a **perfect** or **imperfect cadence**. Name the cadence in each.

DON'T FORGET

A piece of music in binary form has two sections: A and B.

TERNARY FORM (ABA)

A piece of music in **ternary form** divides into *three* sections. We still call these sections **A** and **B**. The difference with ternary form, however, is that section **A** comes back again at the end. We tend to refer to the section at the beginning as **A1** and the section at the end as **A2**. It's important to bear in mind, however, that section A2 does not need to be an exact repeat of A1.

 ACTIVITY

1. Listen to *Volksliedchen (Little Folk-Song)* by Schumann while following the printed melody.

Look out for the sections **A1**, **B** and **A2,** with **B** being a contrasting section.

DON'T FORGET

A piece of music in ternary form has three sections: A1, B and A2.

In ternary form the second section (section B) is generally a contrast to the first section (section A).

contd

50

Forms, styles and periods – Musical forms

2. Listen again to *Volksliedchen (Little Folk-Song)* by Schumann and consider how the composer contrasts sections **A** and **B** in this piece.

For each section, think about concepts that are present in the music under the following headings:

- **Melody/harmony**
- **Rhythm/tempo**
- **Timbre/dynamics**

To focus your listening, choose appropriate concepts from the table.

Melody/harmony	Rhythm/tempo	Timbre/dynamics
Major	Fast	Piano
Minor	Slow	Forte
Grace notes	Minims	Staccato
Perfect cadence	Crotchets	Legato
Imperfect cadence	Quavers	
	Semiquavers	
	Upbeat	
	Downbeat	

THEME AND VARIATIONS

In a **theme and variations,** the composer first introduces the main theme (or tune). The theme is often quite a simple melody, and might not even have been written by the composer. The theme is then repeated many times, but varied in some way each time. This could involve altering the melody, harmony or rhythm; changing the tempo, time signature or tonality; or adding a counter melody or different instruments.

Listen to the second movement of the *Surprise Symphony* by Haydn. This is a **theme and variations** based on the following **binary form** theme:

Section A is in the key of C major. Notice that it modulates to G major towards the end.

Section B returns to C major.

The **variations** are as follows:

1. The second violins and viola play the theme, while the first violins, joined by the flute, add a graceful **countermelody**.
2. Starts **fortissimo** (very loud) in a **minor** key. It then modulates to the **major** key.
3. A repeated note version of bars 1–8 played on the oboe, and then the violins play the theme while the flute and oboe play a duet above them.
4. Woodwind and brass play the theme **fortissimo** to a string accompaniment, with chords played off the beat. Strings and bassoons then play a decorated version of the theme.

The movement ends with a **coda** – loud to begin with, but rounding off the music quietly.

RONDO FORM

If a piece of music is in **rondo form,** the main theme (A) will be heard several times, with contrasting sections of music played in between. These contrasting sections of music are called **episodes**.

A typical plan of a piece of music in rondo form would be:

A1	B	A2	C	A3
The main rondo theme	A contrasting section (episode 1)	The rondo theme again	Another contrasting section (episode 2)	The rondo theme for the last time

Some pieces of music in rondo form have more contrasting sections, so the main rondo theme can sometimes be heard four or more times.

THINGS TO DO AND THINK ABOUT

Listen to the *Rondeau* from *The Fairy Queen* by Purcell, while following the printed music of the main theme. This theme is played twice at the beginning. As you listen, you will hear contrasting sections in between recurrences of this main theme. However, listen out for the main theme returning.

 DON'T FORGET

A piece of music in rondo form has a main theme that comes back three or more times. The contrasting sections of music in between the repeated rondo theme are called episodes.

 ONLINE TEST

Head to www.brightredbooks.net/N5Music to test yourself on musical forms.

51

FORMS, STYLES AND PERIODS

BAROQUE MUSIC 1

In the history of music, different styles have evolved at different periods of time. These styles have their own distinctive sounds and characteristics. It has become accepted to refer to these styles, that evolved before the twentieth century, by the name of the period in which they became established.

The styles that you will need to be familiar with are:

- Baroque
- Classical
- Romantic.

BAROQUE MUSIC

The term **Baroque** is often used to refer to the highly-ornamented style of architecture and art that was fashionable in the seventeenth century. Baroque buildings and paintings were very ornate, and Baroque music often contains **ornaments**.

The harpsichord

A popular instrument associated with Baroque music is the **harpsichord**. You can find out more about the harpsichord on page 48.

Characteristics of Baroque music

Common characteristics of Baroque music include long flowing melodies, often with **sequences** and featuring ornaments.

- A sequence is when a melodic phrase, or pattern, is immediately repeated at a higher or lower pitch.
- An ornament is a way of decorating a melody by adding extra notes. Ornaments can add interest to a melody. Common ornaments include **trills** and **grace notes**.
- **Imitation** is when a melodic idea is immediately copied in another voice or instrument.

EXAMPLE:

Listen to the two-part invention in D minor by J S Bach played on the harpsichord.

Notice that the right hand starts playing on its own for the first two bars. When the left hand starts to play at the third bar, it is copying the melody that was originally played in the right hand, although played an octave lower. This is an example of imitation.

As the music continues, notice that the melodic shape, or pattern, is being repeated at a lower pitch. This is an example of a falling sequence.

As you listen to more of the music, listen out for further sequences as well as ornaments such as trills.

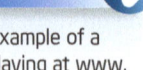 **VIDEO LINK**

Listen to an example of a harpsichord playing at www.brightredbooks.net/N5Music

 DON'T FORGET

The harpsichord was a popular keyboard instrument in Baroque music.

 VIDEO LINK

Head to www.brightredbooks.net/N5Music to listen to the tracks for this section.

 DON'T FORGET

Imitation is when a melodic idea is immediately copied in another voice or instrument.

contd

Forms, styles and periods – Baroque music 1

If a piece of music has two or more melodic lines that are independent of each other, and possibly of equal importance, the texture of the music can be described as either **contrapuntal** or **polyphonic**.

> **EXAMPLE:**
>
> Listen to the opening of the second movement from the *Brandenburg Concerto No. 2* by J S Bach.
>
> Follow the printed music for the first twelve bars as you listen. Against the accompaniment of the cello and harpsichord, notice how three instruments enter one after the other, starting with the same melodic idea, but coming in at different times. This is an example of imitation.
>
> As the music continues, notice how the three instruments continue playing melodic lines quite independently from one another. This creates a contrapuntal or polyphonic texture.
>
>

 DON'T FORGET

A contrapuntal or polyphonic texture is when two or more melodic lines are equally important.

ONLINE TEST

Test yourself on Baroque music at www.brightredbooks.net/N5Music

PEDAL

Another musical device commonly used in Baroque music is a **pedal**. Short for pedal point, a pedal is a note which is sustained, or repeated continuously, in the bass beneath changing harmonies.

Listen to the opening of *Prelude in C* by Bach at www.brightredbooks.net/N5Music, while following the printed music below.

The note in the bass (played by the left hand) is sustained, below the changing outlined chord (played by the right hand). This is the pedal note.

A high-pitched note which is held on or repeated continuously above changing chords is called an **inverted pedal**.

FORMS, STYLES AND PERIODS
BAROQUE MUSIC 2

ONLINE TEST

Test yourself on Baroque music at www.brightredbooks.net/N5Music

VIDEO LINK

Head to www.brightredbooks.net/N5Music to listen to the tracks for this section.

THE VIOLIN

Another popular instrument in **Baroque** music is the **violin**. The **strings** also became the foundation of the Baroque orchestra. The other sections of the orchestra had not yet become fully established.

ACTIVITY

Listen to an excerpt from *Autumn* from *The Four Seasons* by Vivaldi.

Listen for:
- strings
- harpsichord
- 3 beats in the bar
- repetition
- major tonality
- dotted rhythms
- dynamics alternating between loud and soft ('echo' effect).

GROUND BASS

A common structure of Baroque music is the **ground bass**. This is when a theme in the bass is repeated many times while the upper parts are varied.

The *Canon in D* by Pachelbel makes use of the following ground bass:

This bass line is repeated many times by the cellos.

EXAMPLE:

Listen to the opening of *Canon in D* by Pachelbel while following the printed music.

Notice that the three violins come in, one after the other, playing exactly the same melody but just two bars after each other. This very strict type of **imitation** is known as **canon**.

As you listen to the whole piece, notice that the ground bass repeats the same notes all the way through while the string parts become more and more complex.

DON'T FORGET

Keep a record of decisions that you make so that you can come back to that for your composing review.

DON'T FORGET

An **opera** is drama set to music with soloists and chorus, with the actors singing their lines to orchestral accompaniment. It would normally be performed in a theatre.

Another popular keyboard instrument in Baroque music is the **pipe organ**. Composers such as Bach and Handel wrote a great deal of music for the organ. In some Baroque pieces of music you may hear an organ playing along with the strings instead of the harpsichord.

EXAMPLE:

Listen to another version of the *Canon in D* by Pachelbel, featuring the organ instead of the harpsichord.

The ground bass was found not only in instrumental music but also in vocal works of the Baroque period such as opera.

An **aria** is a solo song in an opera.

contd

Forms, styles and periods – Baroque music 2

EXAMPLE:

Listen to the **aria** *Dido's Lament* from the opera *Dido and Aeneas* by Purcell while following the printed music of the first verse. Notice the ground bass in the first five bars. This ground bass repeats throughout the entire aria. The bass line starts off descending in **semitones**. This means that the phrase uses **chromatic** notes.

COMPOSING VARIATIONS ON A GROUND BASS

You are going to create a piece of music built on a ground bass. While you should consider creating your own ground bass, and chord sequence, the following is provided as an example of how you might develop musical ideas in your composition.

Here is an example of a chord sequence with a ground bass:

The following plan may help to give your composition a clear structure. Each step represents four bars of music. However, you might repeat this four-bar phrase many times.

1. Start with the bass line on its own.

The bass line should be repeated many times. If you are using music composing or recording software, you could record the bass line several times, or copy and paste it several times.

2. Add appropriate chords above the bass line, as the bass line repeats.

The chords should also be repeated many times, along with the bass.

You may want to vary the tone of the accompanying chords by trying them out on various instrument sounds.

3. Explore the notes of the chords by playing the individual notes from the chords as crotchets, to give the accompaniment some interest:

4. Experiment with the individual notes of the chords as **broken chords** to vary the rhythm and texture:

5. Create a simple melodic line, or **countermelody**, by using just the notes of the chords:

6. Create a more elaborate melodic line by experimenting with passing notes:

7. Develop your music further by experimenting with melodic features such as **rising sequence** to give a sense of structure to the music:

8. Also try experimenting with a **falling sequence** to provide a sense of balance to the melodic shape:

 ### THINGS TO DO AND THINK ABOUT

Develop your composition further by combining some of your melody and accompaniment ideas to create a more interesting texture; for example, using countermelodies, imitation or different rhythms.

ONLINE TEST

Test yourself on Baroque music at www.brightredbooks.net/N5Music

FORMS, STYLES AND PERIODS

CLASSICAL MUSIC 1

Around the middle of the eighteenth century, the complex **contrapuntal** or **polyphonic** textures of the **Baroque** style began to give way to a more graceful and elegant style of music in which large-scale formal structures were established. This style was known as **Classical** music.

WHAT IS CLASSICAL MUSIC?

The term 'classical' can be a little confusing. Many people use the phrase 'classical music' to refer to any music that isn't based on popular or traditional styles. However, strictly speaking, Classical music refers to a style of music composed approximately between 1750 and 1810. Although a relatively short length of time, in historical terms, the Classical period included the music of Haydn and Mozart and the early compositions of Beethoven. It also saw significant developments in the orchestra, the invention of the piano, and the growth of important musical forms such as the **symphony**, **concerto** and **opera**.

A popular keyboard instrument of the Classical period was the recently invented *pianoforte* – usually called **piano** for short. The piano was invented in Italy by Bartolomeo Cristofori around 1709. He called his new invention the *gravicembalo col piano e forte* – roughly translated as a *keyboard with soft and loud*. Whereas in the harpsichord the strings were plucked, in the new *pianoforte* the strings were struck by hammers. This new mechanism not only created a new sound, but allowed players the ability to vary the dynamic level as well as making a greater contrast between **legato** and **staccato** playing.

A popular musical feature used by Classical composers is the **Alberti bass**, so-called because the Italian composer Domenico Alberti used it extensively. The Alberti bass is a type of repeated broken chord accompaniment played by the left hand on the piano, where the notes of the chord are played in the pattern of low, high, middle, high. This pattern is then repeated for other chords.

This was a very common feature in pieces of music by composers such as Haydn and Mozart.

EXAMPLE:

Listen to the opening of the first movement from *Sonata in C K.545* by Mozart.

Notice the Alberti bass accompaniment in the left hand while the right hand plays the melody.

A common characteristic of Classical music is graceful melodies, in clear-cut and balanced phrases.

EXAMPLE:

Now listen to the opening of the second movement from the same sonata. This movement features clear-cut regular phrases and the Alberti bass throughout. This is very typical of the Classical piano style.

VIDEO LINK

Head to www.brightredbooks.net/N5Music to listen to the tracks for this section.

Forms, styles and periods – Classical music 1

SYMPHONY

The orchestra in the Classical period had was larger than the orchestra in the **Baroque** period. Although it still prominently featured strings, the Classical orchestra often included flutes, oboes, clarinets, bassoons, trumpets, French horns and timpani (kettledrums).

Popular large-scale instrumental forms or styles that became well established during the Classical period were the **symphony** and **concerto**.

The word symphony literally means 'sounding together'.

The symphony is a large-scale work for full orchestra, generally comprising four separate movements, although it is possible to find symphonies with different numbers of movements.

The four movements of a Classical Symphony, contrasted in speed and mood, usually followed the same basic plan:

1. A fairly fast tempo – **Allegro** (sometimes with a slow introduction)
2. A slow tempo – **Andante** or **Adagio** – more lyrical and song-like (often in **ternary form (ABA)** or **theme and variations**).
3. Haydn and Mozart wrote a Minuet and Trio at this point; a bright dance with **3 beats in the bar**. Beethoven later transformed it into a much faster Scherzo.
4. A fast tempo – Allegro, and often light-hearted in mood (commonly structured in **rondo form**).

DON'T FORGET

A symphony is a piece of music played by an orchestra.

ONLINE

Head to www.brightredbooks.net/N5Music for an activity on musical styles.

ONLINE TEST

Test yourself on Classical music at www.brightredbooks.net/N5Music

THINGS TO DO AND THINK ABOUT

Now listen to examples of movements from some different Symphonies.

1. Listen to the first movement from *Symphony No. 29* by Mozart.

   This is fairly typical of the first movement of a Classical symphony with its Allegro tempo and clear-cut phrases. Listen out for the **octave** leaps, which are a prominent feature of the melody at the beginning.

2. Listen to the second movement from *Symphony No. 104* by Haydn.

   Notice the Andante tempo and lyrical song-like melody. The movement opens with strings only, although woodwind and brass join in later on.

3. Listen to the third movement from the *Surprise Symphony* by Haydn.

   This is a lively dance with three beats in the bar. It also starts with an **anacrusis** (i.e. an **upbeat**).

4. Listen to the fourth movement from *Symphony No. 5* by Beethoven.

   This movement opens with the full orchestra, in a **major** key. The same movement finishes with a rather extended **coda,** keeping the listener waiting for when the piece is going to end.

FORMS, STYLES AND PERIODS

CLASSICAL MUSIC 2

CONCERTO

The **concerto** is a large-scale work for a solo instrument and orchestra, generally with three movements. Many concertos were composed throughout the Baroque, Classical and Romantic periods.

An important feature of a concerto is the **cadenza**. A cadenza is a 'showy' passage in the music designed to give the soloist the opportunity to demonstrate their musical technique. It is played without orchestral accompaniment and often ends with a trill, as a signal to the orchestra to play again.

The three movements of a typical concerto, contrasted in speed and mood, generally followed the same basic plan:

1. A fairly fast tempo – **Allegro;** during this movement, there is usually a cadenza.
2. A slow tempo – **Andante** or **Adagio** – more lyrical and song-like (often in **ternary form (ABA)** or **theme and variations**).
3. A fast tempo – Allegro, and often light-hearted in mood (commonly structured in **rondo form**).

Notice that the three movements of a concerto are like the movements of a **symphony**, but without the Minuet/Scherzo and Trio.

Now listen to examples of movements from some different concertos.

EXAMPLE:

Listen to the first movement from the *Piano Concerto No. 23 in A major* by Mozart.

You will hear the orchestra playing, but you will hear the piano featured as a soloist. You can also hear a good example of a cadenza towards the end of the movement (the cadenza starts approximately 8 minutes and 25 seconds into the movement).

EXAMPLE:

Listen to the third movement from the *Horn Concerto No. 4* by Mozart.

This movement is in rondo form, which means that the main theme (A) is heard several times, with contrasting sections of music played in between. These contrasting sections are called **episodes**.

The overall structure, therefore, is **A B A C A** and follows the typical rondo form plan:

A1	B	A2	C	A3
The main rondo theme	A contrasting section (episode 1)	The rondo theme again	Another contrasting section (episode 2)	The rondo theme for the last time

Here is the printed music of the main rondo theme:

This theme is played at the beginning by the French horn and is immediately repeated by the rest of the orchestra. As you listen, you will hear contrasting sections (episodes). However, listen out for the main rondo theme returning.

ACTIVITY

As you listen to the third movement from the *Horn Concerto No. 4* by Mozart, consider the following questions:

Is the music in **simple time** or **compound time**?

The music does not start on the first beat of the bar. Which concept is used to describe this?

VIDEO LINK

Head to www.brightredbooks.net/N5Music to listen to the tracks for this section.

Forms, styles and periods – Classical music 2

COMPOSING A THEME AND VARIATIONS

Theme and variations is one of the oldest musical structures and can be applied to any style of music. The basic idea is that you choose a theme, either a melody that you have composed or a melody that you have borrowed from somewhere else (e.g. a folk-song, a popular song, a nursery rhyme, a 'classical' piece etc.).

The theme is first presented in a relatively straightforward manner. The music is then developed by repeating the theme several times, but each time varying it or altering it in some way. The number of ways in which a theme can be varied is countless. It's entirely up to the composer.

Look at the opening of the melody *Twinkle Twinkle Little Star*:

The melody is very simple.

Now consider some simple composing techniques that could be used to develop this melody.

Decoration – keeping the outline of the melody and adding extra notes between the main melody notes:

Syncopation – altering the rhythm to make it sound more interesting or to give the melody a 'jazzy' feel:

Change of time signature – from 4 beats in the bar to 3 beats in the bar:

Change in tonality – playing the music in a minor key instead of a major key:

THINGS TO DO AND THINK ABOUT

Here are some techniques that you could explore and experiment with to develop your composition.

Melody/harmony:
- Decorate the theme with **ornaments, trills** or passing notes.
- Change the **tonality** (from **major** to **minor**, or minor to major).
- Take the theme, or part of the theme, and experiment with concepts such as **sequence** or **chromatic** notes.
- Take the melody away altogether and keep the original **harmony**.
- Create a new melody over the original harmony.
- A **countermelody** could be added either above or below the theme.

Rhythm/tempo:
- Change the **tempo** (speed).
- Experiment with different rhythms (e.g. add **dotted notes** or use **syncopation**).
- Change the **time signature** (i.e. the number of beats in the bar).

Texture/structure/form:
- Put the theme into the **bass**, or an inner part.
- Add an **Alberti bass** pattern.
- Experiment with techniques such as **canon** or **imitation** to create a **polyphonic** or **contrapuntal** texture.

Timbre/dynamics
- Consider which instrument you would like to play the melody.
- Consider other instruments that you may want to accompany the melody.
- Explore different string playing techniques such as **arco** or **pizzicato**.

DON'T FORGET
A concerto is a piece of music featuring a solo instrument and orchestra.

ONLINE TEST
Test yourself on Classical music at www.brightredbooks.net/N5Music

DON'T FORGET
Keep a record of decisions that you make so that you can come back to it for your composing review.

DON'T FORGET
Make a short list of what you think works well in your composition.

DON'T FORGET
Make a short list of what you could do to improve your composition.

FORMS, STYLES AND PERIODS

ROMANTIC MUSIC

The nineteenth-century Romantic Movement was a period in history when artists, writers and composers deliberately attempted to convey intense emotions and express personal ideas, often influenced by historical events, political issues and nature.

CHARACTERISTICS OF ROMANTIC MUSIC

Common characteristics of **Romantic** music include extended melodies, often using a lot of **chromatic** notes and chords (i.e. using semitones), a greater freedom in form, more adventurous modulations, and a wider range of dynamics. The music tended to be very expressive, conveying strong emotions.

Romantic music also sometimes features the use of **rubato**. This is when a performer changes the tempo of a piece of music slightly, for more expression.

VIDEO LINK

Head to www.brightredbooks.net/N5Music to listen to the tracks for this section.

EXAMPLE:

Listen to *First Loss* Op. 68 No. 16 by Schumann played on the piano. The melody for the first section is printed below.

This is a short character piece intended to express feelings of melancholy.

ACTIVITY

As you listen to *First Loss*, consider the following questions:

Does the music start on the first beat of the bar or does it start with an **anacrusis**?

Does the music sound **major** or **minor**?

Does the music maintain a steady pulse throughout or is there any **rubato**?

Many composers in the Romantic period composed short piano pieces for amateur musicians to play. Some of these short pieces had descriptive titles and were intended to convey a particular mood or character.

Examples of these include:

- *Elfentanz* Op.12 No. 4 from *Lyric Pieces* by Grieg
- *Träumerei* Op. 15 No. 7 by Schumann
- *Nocturne in E flat* Op. 9 No. 2 by Chopin.

ACTIVITY

As you listen to these other short piano pieces, consider the same questions for each one:

1. How does the composer convey mood or character in the music?
2. Does the music start on the first beat of the bar or does it start with an anacrusis?
3. Does the music sound major or minor?
4. Does the music maintain a steady pulse throughout or is there any rubato?

contd

Forms, styles and periods – Romantic music

The **orchestra** became much larger in the Romantic period, with the addition of more **woodwind**, **brass** and **percussion** instruments, such as the **piccolo**, **trombone** and **snare drum**, and an increase in the numbers of **string** players. This resulted in very expressive and descriptive orchestral works, sometimes inspired by nature.

EXAMPLE:

Listen to the first minute or two of *The Hebrides Overture* by Mendelssohn.

On a visit to Scotland in 1829, the 20-year-old Mendelssohn came across the caverns on the island of Staffa in the Inner Hebrides. Inspired by its rugged beauty, Mendelssohn composed *The Hebrides Overture* (also known as *Fingal's Cave*).

The piece begins straight away with a very prominent repeating theme played by the violas, cellos and bassoons, portraying the murmur of the sea and the roll of the waves towards the mouth of the cave.

As you listen, try to identify the following prominent features in the music, under the given headings.

Melody/harmony	Rhythm/tempo	Instruments	Dynamics
Minor tonality	4 beats in the bar	Clarinets	Piano
Repetition	Allegro moderato	Bassoons	Forte
Sequences		Violins	Crescendo
Countermelody		Violas	
		Cellos	
		Strings	
		Tremolando	
		Timpani (roll)	

Romantic music is generally very expressive, conveying feelings and emotions.

Romantic music often uses a wide range of dynamics.

Rubato is an Italian term to describe a performer changing the tempo of a piece of music slightly, to make it sound more expressive.

Which concept is used to describe a performer slightly varying the tempo of a piece of music for expressive effect?

THINGS TO DO AND THINK ABOUT

To help you revise the important features of **Baroque, Classical** and Romantic music, you should produce a short summary of the music concepts associated with each of these three styles, and also identify one or two pieces of music from each style that contain these concepts. The summaries don't have to be in the style of an essay, but should identify the most important concepts. You could, for example, create a mind map for each style, produce an electronic presentation for each style, or simply compile a list of bullet points.

To show that you fully understand each style, you should identify appropriate concepts under the following headings:

- style
- rhythm/tempo
- timbre/dynamics.
- melody/harmony
- texture/structure/form

Then, to put your understanding of the styles into a musical context, identify one or two pieces of music from each style that contain the concepts you have identified.

Test yourself on Romantic music at www.brightredbooks.net/N5Music

TWENTIETH-CENTURY MUSIC

IMPRESSIONIST MUSIC

During the twentieth century a wide range of musical styles emerged. While some composers adopted quite a traditional approach to music, others took a very experimental approach.

THE DEVELOPMENT OF IMPRESSIONIST MUSIC

A style of music that developed in the early part of the twentieth century was called Impressionist music. The term Impressionist was borrowed from a style of painting in which the images were blurred and hazy.

Impression, sunrise (1873) by Monet

Early-twentieth-century Impressionist composers, such as Claude Debussy and Maurice Ravel, attempted to incorporate the same vague, hazy feelings into their music. While Impressionist music is not a style that you will be required to know for the National 5 exam, an important melodic concept associated with Impressionist music is the **whole-tone scale**.

WHOLE-TONE SCALE

A common feature of Impressionist music is the use of the whole-tone scale.

The whole-tone scale is made up from notes that are a tone apart.

Here are the notes of the whole-tone scale, starting on middle C:

C　D　E　F#　G#　A#　(C)

contd

Twentieth-century music – Impressionist music

If you look at a keyboard you will notice that the whole-tone scale gets its name from the fact that it contains only **tones** and avoids the use of **semitones**.

Music based on a whole-tone scale can sound rather mysterious or magical.

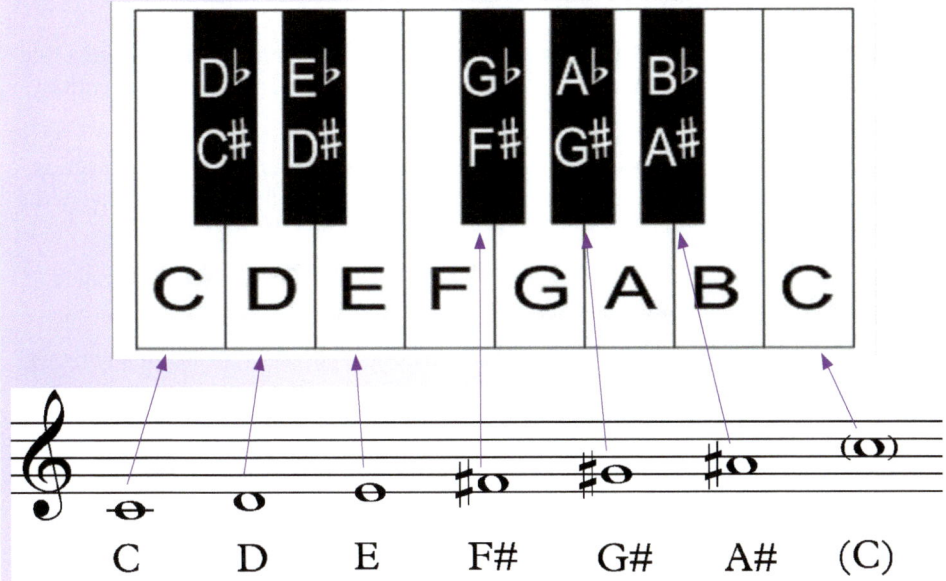

VIDEO LINK

Listen to the opening of *Cloches à travers les feuilles* by Debussy at www.brightredbooks.net/N5Music. This is an example of Impressionist music, making clear use of the whole-tone scale at the beginning.

ATONAL MUSIC

Some composers in the twentieth century felt that tonality (i.e. music being in either a major or a minor key) had become too limiting. So, they started to experiment with **atonal** music.

Atonal music is music that has no sense of being in a particular key. A common feature of atonal music is the use of **discords**. This is when two or more notes are played together that clash. Atonal music also often features large intervals and short melodic fragments.

Listen to No. 1 of the *Six Little Piano Pieces* by Arnold Schoenberg at www.brightredbooks.net/N5Music. As you listen, notice the following:

- The music is atonal and contains many discords.
- There are a number of wide leaps.

DON'T FORGET

Atonal music is music that has no sense of being in either a major or minor key.

CLUSTER

Listen to *The Tides of Manaunaun* by Henry Cowell at www.brightredbooks.net/N5Music. This features clusters being played on the piano.

A **cluster** is a group of notes, all next to one another, played at the same time, creating a clash in the harmony. Sometimes a cluster can be played on a keyboard instrument with the palm of the hand or even with the forearm.

ONLINE TEST

Test yourself on twentieth-century music at www.brightredbooks.net/N5Music

THINGS TO DO AND THINK ABOUT

Familiarise yourself with the notes of the whole-tone scale on your chosen instrument.

Experiment with the notes, and get familiar with the sound of the scale.

Try composing a short melody using only the notes of the whole-tone scale.

TWENTIETH-CENTURY MUSIC

MINIMALIST MUSIC

WHAT IS MINIMALIST MUSIC?

Minimalist music is a style of music based on simple melodic and rhythmic figures that are repeated many times with slight changes. Complete pieces are often based entirely on short repeated phrases.

This style evolved during the second half of the twentieth century, partly as a reaction against some of the highly complex and **atonal** music that had been so influential in the early part of the century.

Minimalist composers, such as Terry Riley, Philip Glass and John Adams, deliberately attempted to make their music simpler and more accessible to the listener.

In C by Terry Riley consists of a number of short musical phrases repeated many times. It illustrates another common feature of Minimalist music – the overlaying of different melodic lines and rhythm patterns.

While the overlaying of different melodic lines can create a more complex texture, the overlaying of different rhythm patterns is known as **cross rhythms**.

Cross rhythms occur when two or more rhythmic patterns are played at the same time by different parts or instruments.

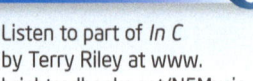

Listen to part of *In C* by Terry Riley at www.brightredbooks.net/N5Music.

Listen to the opening of *Glassworks* by Philip Glass at www.brightredbooks.net/N5Music. This piece contains examples of simple melodic and harmonic ideas, **repetition** and cross rhythms.

COMPOSING A MINIMALIST PIECE

The following steps provide some examples of techniques that you could experiment with to develop a composition in a Minimalist style.

1. Start by creating a short musical motif. Keep it simple, possibly containing just four or five notes. For example:

2. Now repeat the motif several times, keeping the rhythm simple.

   Here is the motif above extended into regular groups of four quavers:

3. Repeat the motif, developing it further by experimenting with slight changes to the rhythmic pattern. For example, in the midst of groups of four quavers you might include an occasional group of three quavers:

contd

Twentieth-century music – Minimalist music

4. Then you might add a second part, experimenting with the use of **contrary motion**.

   This means that the lower part will move in the opposite direction to the upper part:

5. To create a slightly more complex texture you could explore different rhythm patterns and experiment with adding another part using **cross rhythms**. In this example the upper part has groups of four quavers while the lower part has dotted crotchets:

ACTIVITY

Compose a short Minimalist piece of music based on the above ideas.

Experiment with different groupings of notes (e.g. groups of five or six).

Using a computer, with a music composing or sequencing programme, try to develop your composition by overlaying several lines of music using cross rhythms.

DON'T FORGET

Minimalist music is based on a lot of repetition, although often the repeating pattern changes slightly.

DON'T FORGET

A cluster is a group of notes, all next to one another, played at the same time.

ONLINE TEST

Test yourself on Minimalist music at www.brightredbooks.net/N5Music

THINGS TO DO AND THINK ABOUT

To help you revise the different styles of twentieth-century music, you should produce a short summary of the music concepts associated with each style, and also identify one or two pieces of music from each style that contain these concepts. The summary could be in the style of a written report, a mind map, an electronic presentation, or simply a list of bullet points.

To show that you fully understand each twentieth-century style, you should identify concepts under the following headings:

- style
- rhythm/tempo
- timbre/dynamics.
- melody/harmony
- texture/structure/form

Then, to put your understanding of the styles into a musical context, identify one or two pieces of music from each style that contain the concepts you have identified.

MUSIC LITERACY

CONCEPTS AND MELODY/HARMONY

Music literacy is about understanding music notation. You will explore many of the music literacy concepts through performing music, listening to music and creating your own music.

ONLINE

Head to www.brightredbooks.net/N5Music for exercises on music literacy.

CONCEPTS

The music literacy concepts in the National 5 Music course build on previous knowledge and understanding of music concepts at lower levels. This means that you will be expected to have a secure understanding of the music literacy concepts at National 3 and National 4 levels, in addition to knowledge and understanding of the National 5 music literacy concepts.

These three tables list all the music literacy concepts that you would be required to know for National 3, National 4 and National 5 Music.

Melody/harmony	Rhythm/tempo	Timbre/dynamics
Lines and spaces of the treble clef	Crotchet	**f** – forte
Steps	Minim	**p** – piano
Repetition	Dotted minim	**< cresc** – crescendo
	Semibreve	**> dim** – diminuendo
	Bar lines	
	Double bar lines	

Music literacy concepts for **National 3**

Melody/harmony	Rhythm/tempo	Timbre/dynamics
Treble clef stave C–A'	Quaver	**mf** – mezzo forte
Sequences	Semiquaver	**mp** – mezzo piano
	Grouped semiquavers	
	Paired quavers	
	Repeat signs	

Music literacy concepts for **National 4**

Melody/harmony	Rhythm/tempo	Timbre/dynamics
Tones	Dotted rhythms	**ff** — fortissimo
Semitones	Dotted crotchet	**pp** — pianissimo
Accidentals: flats, sharps and naturals	Dotted quaver	**sfz** — sforzando
Scales and key signatures: C major, G major, F major and A minor	Scotch snap	
Chords: C major, G major, F major and A minor	1st and 2nd time bars	
Leaps		

Music literacy concepts for **National 5**

DON'T FORGET

For the National 5 Music course you will need to know all the music concepts for National 3, National 4 and National 5.

This section provides an overview of all the music literacy concepts required at each level by category, for example, **melody/harmony, rhythm/tempo** and **timbre/dynamics**.

MELODY/HARMONY

In music notation notes are written on five lines and four spaces called a stave or a staff.

For most melody instruments, there will be a sign called a treble clef at the beginning of the stave.

Treble clef

Lines and spaces of the treble clef

The treble clef indicates that the lines and spaces have particular names. The lines and spaces on the treble clef are named after the first seven letters of the alphabet, and correspond to the notes that would be played on an instrument, or sung.

The five lines of the treble clef are:

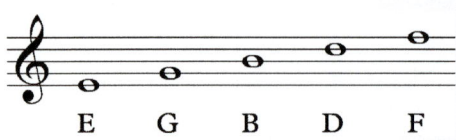

E G B D F

The four spaces of the treble clef are:

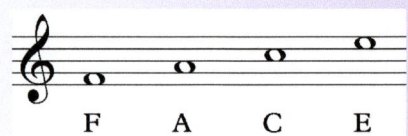

F A C E

contd

Music literacy – Concepts and melody/harmony

Treble clef stave C–A'

The notes that you will be expected to know on the treble clef are those from middle C (below the stave) to high A (above the stave).

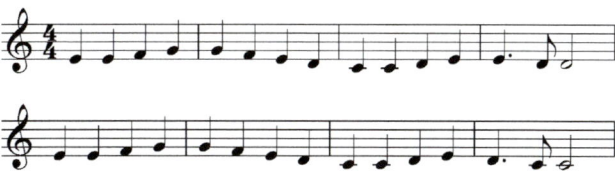

Steps

When the notes of a melody are moving up or down between notes which are next to each other, the melody is said to be moving by **step**.

Here is part of *Ode To Joy* by Beethoven. Notice that the melody moves entirely by step.

Leaps

When the notes of a melody are moving up or down between notes which are not next to each other, the melody is said to be moving by **leap**.

Here is part of *The Last Post*. Notice that the melody moves entirely by leap.

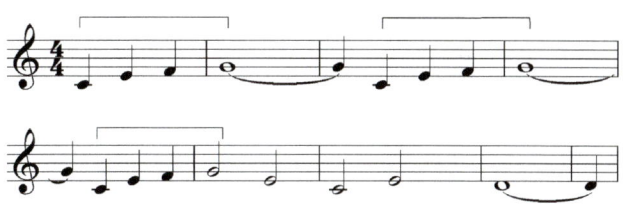

Repetition

Repetition is when a musical phrase or idea is played more than once.

Here is part of *Oh When The Saints Go Marching In*. Notice that the first group of four notes (shown by the bracket) is played three times. This is an example of repetition.

Sequences

A **sequence** is a melodic phrase which is immediately repeated at either a higher or lower pitch.

Here is part of *Angels We Have Heard On High*. Notice that the first pattern of notes is repeated a step lower each time. This is an example of a sequence.

Accidentals (flats, sharps and naturals)

Accidentals are signs that come in front of a note and alter the pitch of the note. The table shows the signs for a **flat**, a **sharp** and a **natural**, and provides a description of what effect each would have on a note.

Accidentals should always be written in front of the note, very clearly on the appropriate line or in the appropriate space, as shown.

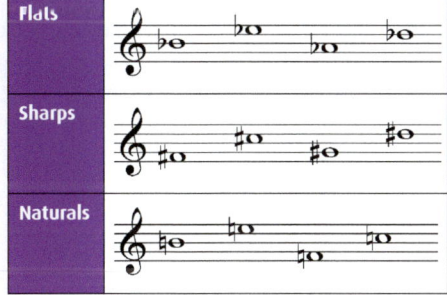

Flat	♭	A flat sign in front of a note lowers the pitch of the note by a semitone.
Sharp	♯	A sharp sign in front of a note raises the pitch of the note by a semitone.
Natural	♮	A natural sign in front of a note cancels out any previous flat or sharp and restores the note to its original pitch.

THINGS TO DO AND THINK ABOUT

Use the concepts tables on page 66 as a checklist of all the music literacy concepts you need to know. This will help you to identify all the concepts that you already know, and let you see which concepts you might not be so sure of.

ONLINE TEST

Test yourself on music literacy at www.brightredbooks.net/N5Music

MUSIC LITERACY

MORE ON MELODY/HARMONY

TONES AND SEMITONES

A **semitone** is the smallest distance between any two notes.

On a keyboard, there is a semitone between the notes E and F, and between the notes B and C. This is because there are no black notes in between. There would also be a semitone between any black and white notes next to one another. For example, there is a semitone between the notes F# and G, and between the notes B and B♭.

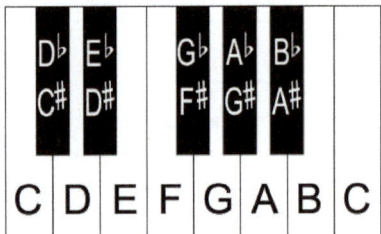

A tone is the equivalent of two semitones. Therefore, there is a **tone** between the notes C and D, between the notes E and F#, and between the notes B♭ and A♭.

Notice that the black notes can all have two possible names, as a flat or as a sharp. For example, an F# is the same note as a G♭, and a B♭ is the same note as an A#.

Examples of notes that are a semitone apart:

Examples of notes that are a tone (i.e. two semitones) apart:

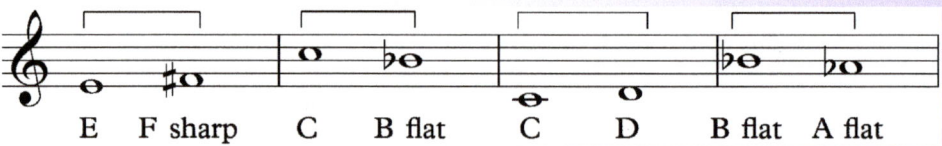

SCALES AND KEY SIGNATURES (C MAJOR, G MAJOR, F MAJOR AND A MINOR)

The key of a piece of music is indicated by a **key signature**. The key signature is indicated by the sharps or flats at the beginning of a piece of music. There are four keys that you should be able to recognise for National 5 Music. These are C major, G major, F major and A minor. The table below gives the name of each key, shows the key signature and provides a description of the key signature.

Key	Key signature	Description
C major and A minor	(treble clef, no sharps or flats)	The key signatures of both C major and A minor have no sharps or flats. However, in the key of A minor you would expect to see some G sharps in either the melody or the harmony. See the sections on scales and chords below.
G major	(treble clef with one sharp)	The key signature of G major has one sharp (F sharp). The F sharp is always written on the top line of the treble clef, and appears at the beginning of every stave.
F major	(treble clef with one flat)	The key signature of F major has one flat (B flat). The B flat is always written on the middle line of the treble clef, and appears at the beginning of every stave.

A **scale** is a series of notes moving by step in either an ascending or descending order.

For National 5 Music, you should be able to recognise scales in the keys of C major, G major, F major and A minor.

contd

Music literacy – More on melody/harmony

The scale of C major:

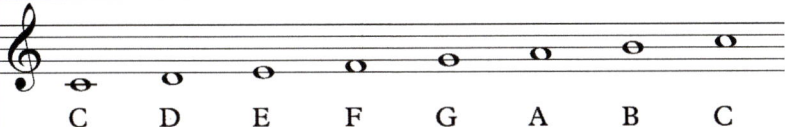

The scale of G major:

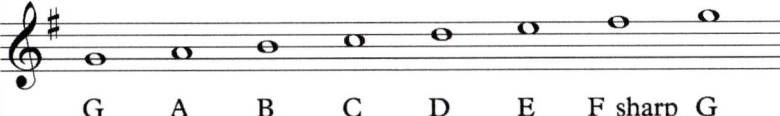

The scale of F major:

The scale of A minor:

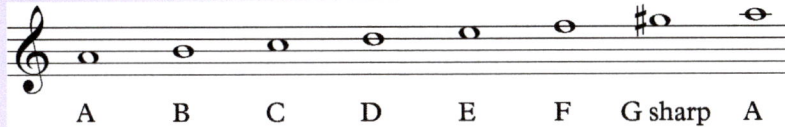

Notice that the scale of A minor contains a G sharp as an accidental.

DON'T FORGET
There are only four keys that you will be expected to recognise in the National 5 Music question paper: C major, G major, F major and A minor.

ONLINE
Head to www.brightredbooks.net/N5Music for exercises on music literacy.

ONLINE TEST
Test yourself on music literacy at www.brightredbooks.net/N5Music

CHORDS (C MAJOR, G MAJOR, F MAJOR AND A MINOR)

You will also need to be able to recognise chords in the keys of C major, G major, F major and A minor. The table shows the common chords in each of these four keys. In each case the chord name is printed above each chord (e.g. C, F, G and Am). It is common practice to use the lowercase letter 'm' to indicate a **minor** chord. Therefore, Am is a common abbreviation for the chord of A minor. The chord number is also printed below each chord (e.g. I, IV, V and VI). It is common practice to use Roman numerals to indicate the number of a chord. This refers to the degree (or note) of the scale on which the chord is based. For example; in the key of C major the chord of C is called chord I because it is based on the first note of the scale, the chord of F is called chord IV because it is based on the fourth note of the scale, the chord of G is called chord V because it is based on the fifth note of the scale, and the chord of Am (A minor) is called chord VI because it is based on the sixth note of the scale.

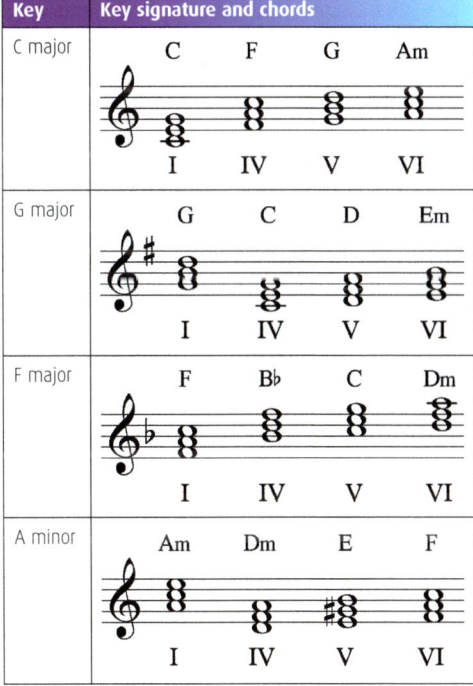

THINGS TO DO AND THINK ABOUT

Look at a piece of music that you are performing and try to identify the key of the music.

Look at the melody of a piece of music that you are performing and try to identify any tones or semitones.

MUSIC LITERACY

RHYTHM/TEMPO AND TIMBRE/DYNAMICS

RHYTHM/TEMPO

Bar lines and double bar lines

Printed music is divided into small section called bars. Each bar adds up to an equal number of beats and are separated by vertical lines called **bar lines**. The end of a piece of music is indicated by a **double bar line**. Sometimes the end of a section of music will also have a double bar line.

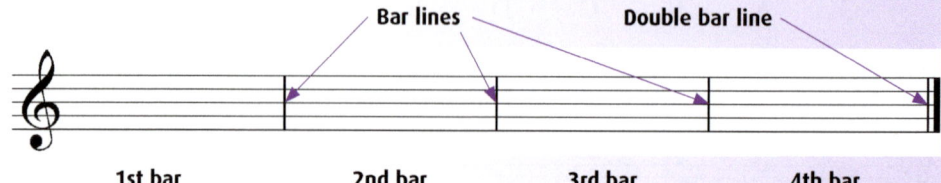

DON'T FORGET

The time signature should be written immediately after the treble clef and any key signature, but before the first note of the music.

ONLINE

Test yourself on Music Literacy at www.brightredbooks.net/N5Music

Time signatures

A **time signature** is formed by the two numbers at the beginning of a piece of music. In general, the top number tells you how many beats there are in each bar and the bottom number tells you what kind of beats they are. Crotchet beats are indicated by the number 4 at the bottom.

In **simple time** each beat can be divided into two. The table below has examples of time signatures in **simple time**, showing how they would appear at the beginning of a piece of music, along with a description of each.

In **compound time** each beat can be divided into three. The table below has examples of time signatures in **compound time**, showing how they would appear at the beginning of a piece of music, along with a description of each.

Simple time

Time signature	Description
2/4	Two crotchet beats in every bar
3/4	Three crotchet beats in every bar
4/4	Four crotchet beats in every bar
C	Common time – an alternative way of indicating four crotchet beats in every bar

Compound time

Time signature	Description
6/8	Two dotted crotchet beats in every bar
9/8	Three dotted crotchet beats in every bar
12/8	Four dotted crotchet beats in every bar

Note values

As well as knowing which notes to play, a performer also needs to know how many beats each note should last. Remember that a dot placed after a note adds half the value of the original note. The table shows all the notes you will need to know, along with the name of each note, and the number of beats each note lasts for.

Note	Name	Length
𝅝	Semibreve	4 beats
𝅗𝅥.	Dotted minim	3 beats
𝅗𝅥	Minim	2 beats
𝅘𝅥.	Dotted crotchet	1½ beats
𝅘𝅥	Crotchet	1 beat
𝅘𝅥𝅮.	Dotted quaver	¾ beat
𝅘𝅥𝅮	Quaver	½ beat
𝅘𝅥𝅯	Semiquaver	¼ beat

Rhythmic groupings

There are conventions for grouping notes together.

For example, in melodies that have quavers, it is common practice for the quavers to be beamed together in twos, threes or fours, depending on the time signature. When dotted notes are used, it is common to have a longer note and a shorter note together to make up either one or two full beats. The table illustrates some common groupings of notes, along with a description of each grouping.

Notes	Grouping	Description
	Paired quavers	Two quavers beamed together
	Grouped quavers	Four quavers beamed together
	Grouped quavers	Three quavers beamed together (usually found in compound time)
	Grouped semiquavers	Four semiquavers beamed together
	Dotted rhythm	Dotted crotchet followed by a quaver (adding up to two beats)
	Dotted rhythm	Dotted quaver followed by a semiquaver (adding up to one beat)
	Scotch snap	Semiquaver followed by a dotted quaver (adding up to one beat)

DON'T FORGET

Remember to use music literacy concepts in your composing assignment, to create your score, as well as trying to identify some in pieces of music that you are either performing or listening to.

contd

Music literacy – Rhythm/tempo and timbre/dynamics

Repeat signs

A repeat sign is a double bar line with two dots in the middle two spaces, indicating that a section of music should be played again. This is known as an End Repeat.

A corresponding sign facing the other way can also be used, indicating where the repeat is to begin. This is known as a Start Repeat.

Here is part of a French folk-song. Notice the repeat sign at the end, indicating that the melody should be played again from the beginning.

If you are required to simply repeat a section of the music, rather than going back to the very beginning, the Start Repeat sign would be used to indicate where to repeat from. Here is part of the same French folk-song. Notice the repeat signs at both the beginning and the end, indicating where the music should be repeated from.

First and second time bars

When a section of music is repeated, but with a different ending, numbered brackets are placed above the appropriate bars indicating which ending to play the first time and which to play the second time. These are called first and second time bars or first and second time endings.

The first time ending bracket will appear above the bar that has to be played the first time:

During the second playing, the notes in the first time ending would be missed out.

The second time ending bracket will appear above the bar that has to be played the second time:

Here is part of *Ode To Joy* by Beethoven, using first and second time endings. Notice the slightly different ending, indicated by the first and second time bars.

Italian terms

Composers often use Italian terms to indicate the tempo or character of the music. The table gives the Italian terms regarding tempo that you will need to know, along with their meanings.

Italian term	Meaning
Adagio	Slow
Andante	A walking speed (moderately slow)
Moderato	A moderate or medium speed
Allegro	Fast
Rubato	Slight variation in speed
Accelerando (*accel.*)	Gradually getting faster
Rallentando (*rall.*)	Gradually getting slower
Ritardando (*rit.*)	Gradually getting slower
A tempo	Return to the original speed, after there has been a change

TIMBRE/DYNAMICS

In music notation, it is common to find different Italian terms (or abbreviations), as well as other signs, to indicate the dynamic level (i.e. the volume level) of the music.

The table gives Italian terms for dynamics that you will need to know, along with the appropriate abbreviations and meanings.

Italian term	Abbreviation	Meaning
fortissimo	ff	Very loud
forte	f	Loud
mezzo forte	mf	Moderately loud
mezzo piano	mp	Moderately quiet
piano	p	Quiet
pianissimo	pp	Very quiet
sforzando	sfz	Played with force, or a sudden accent

In some cases, a composer may require a gradual change in volume level. The table below gives two Italian terms, abbreviations and signs, commonly used to indicate a change in dynamics.

Italian term	Abbreviation	Sign	Meaning
crescendo	cresc.	&lt;	Getting gradually louder
diminuendo	dim.	&gt;	Getting gradually quieter

THINGS TO DO AND THINK ABOUT

Look at pieces of music that you are performing and try to identify some music literacy concepts such as the key signature and time signature; Italian terms or abbreviations about the tempo or dynamics; repeat signs or first and second time endings; dotted rhythms or other rhythmic groupings.

COURSE ASSESSMENT

QUESTION PAPER

COURSE ASSESSMENT

This section will provide you with more detailed information about the four externally assessed components, along with advice on how to prepare for each of them. The National 5 Music course consists of four components, all of which are externally assessed.

The following table provides a summary of the four components, showing how each one will be assessed, and indicating the marks available:

The course assessment will provide the basis for the final grade awarded (for example, A, B, C or D). Your grade will be based on the total percentage for all four course assessment components added together (i.e. the scaled marks for the question paper, the composing assignment and performance on both instruments, or one instrument and voice).

This National 5 Music Study Guide will provide you with a range of practical activities to help you develop your skills in listening, composing and performing, and practical advice about preparing for the listening question paper, the composing assignment and the performance exam.

Component	How it will be assessed	Marks available	Scaled mark
Question Paper	Written examination based on listening to excerpts of music	40	35%
Composing Assignment	Submission of a completed composition	30	15%
Performance - Instrument 1	Live performance marked by a visiting assessor	30	25%
Performance - Instrument 2	Live performance marked by a visiting assessor	30	25%

OVERVIEW OF THE QUESTION PAPER

You will have a final exam in the form of a question paper. The exam, which will last approximately forty-five minutes, is based on listening to excerpts of music and answering questions on what you hear. The question paper is marked out of 40, and will then be scaled to a mark out of 35, meaning that it will be worth 35% of your course award.

The purpose of the question paper is to test your knowledge and understanding of music concepts and music literacy. You will demonstrate your knowledge and understanding of music concepts by answering questions based on a variety of excerpts from different styles. A range of question types will be used in the question paper, covering a variety of music concepts including music literacy. All the questions in the question paper are compulsory.

This section will provide you with advice on how to revise for the question paper, and show examples of types of questions you will come across in the question paper.

TOPICS TO REVISE

The questions in the exam will test your knowledge and understanding of music concepts from styles that you have covered throughout your course, such as:

- Scottish music
- World music
- Vocal music
- Instrumental music
- Popular music styles
- Baroque, Classical and Romantic music
- Twentieth-century music.

Some of the questions in the exam will also test your knowledge and understanding of other aspects of music, including:

- identifying musical instruments and groups
- methods of producing sound on different instruments
- Italian terms (for tempo, dynamics and playing techniques)
- music literacy.

QUESTION STYLES

The questions in the exam will be in a variety of formats, including:

- multiple choice questions
- writing short answers (single words or short phrases)
- identifying chord changes
- music guide
- music literacy (involving music notation)
- inserting concepts in a text
- identifying prominent features.

Examples of how these questions will look, along with advice on how to answer the questions, can be found below.

MULTIPLE CHOICE QUESTIONS

The multiple choice questions simply ask you to tick one or more boxes to identify what you hear in the music. The number of available marks will always indicated at the right hand side of the page. As a general rule, there will be one mark available for each correct answer.

Some multiple choice questions will ask you to choose **one** answer from a choice of four options.

For example, a question asking you to identify a style will look something like this:

(a) Listen to this excerpt and tick **one** box to identify what you hear.
- [ ] Gospel
- [ ] Ragtime
- [ ] Reggae
- [ ] Indian

Another question may ask you to identify a feature from an unrelated range of concepts:

c) Listen to this excerpt and tick **one** box to identify what you hear.
- [ ] A cappella
- [ ] Ground bass
- [ ] Flutter tonguing
- [ ] Grace notes

A question asking you to identify a Scottish dance might look something like this:

(b) Listen to this excerpt and tick **one** box to identify what you hear.
- [ ] Waltz
- [ ] Strathspey
- [ ] Reel
- [ ] Jig

Another multiple choice question will ask you to identify **two** concepts from a choice of five options. For example:

(d) Listen to this excerpt and tick **two** boxes to identify what you hear.
- [ ] Soprano
- [ ] Tenor
- [ ] Bass
- [ ] Syllabic
- [ ] Melismatic

GIVE A REASON FOR YOUR ANSWER

Some multiple choice questions, asking you to identify a style, will have a follow-up question asking you to give a reason to support your answer, as in the example shown.

When giving a reason to support your answer, you should identify an appropriate concept in the music that relates to the style e.g. if the style is Indian, your reason might be sitar or tabla. If the style is Jig, your reason might be compound time. If the style is Ragtime, your reason might be syncopation. If the style is Baroque, your reason might be harpsichord or ornaments.

Make sure you know which concepts or features relate to particular styles.

(a) As you listen to this excerpt:
  (i) tick **one** box to identify the style of the music, and
  (ii) in the space below, give a reason to support your answer

- [ ] Indian
- [ ] Jig
- [ ] Ragtime
- [ ] Baroque

Reason: _____

COURSE ASSESSMENT

MORE ON THE QUESTION PAPER

WRITING SHORT ANSWERS

Some questions require you to write one or two words or a short phrase. Note that sometimes you will be required to write an Italian term. Examples of these types of questions are as follows:

(a) Listen to the following excerpt. Name the solo instrument playing.
_____

(b) Listen to a new excerpt and write the Italian term to describe the string playing technique.
_____

(c) Listen to a further excerpt. Identify the style of the music.
_____

DON'T FORGET

Read the question carefully. There is generally a clue to the answer in the wording of the question.

DON'T FORGET

This type of question may ask you to identify an instrument (or group of instruments), or a type of voice.

DON'T FORGET

Sometimes you will be asked to write an appropriate Italian term.

DON'T FORGET

Remember: your answer must always be a music concept.

CHORD CHANGES

In this question you will be asked to tick **one** box to identify the chord sequence heard in a song. The chords used will be **I, IV, V** and **VI** in a major key. It is the convention to use Roman numerals for chord numbers, although the actual chord names will also be given. You will also be told the key of the music. Here is an example of how this question will look:

Tick **one** box to identify the chord sequence heard in this song.
The music is in the key of C major.
You will hear the excerpt twice, with a pause of 10 seconds between playings.

I	V	VI	IV
C	G	Am	F

I	VI	IV	V
C	Am	F	G

I	IV	V	VI
C	F	G	Am

DON'T FORGET

Listen carefully to the bass notes (i.e. the lowest notes). The bass note is often the root note of the chord.

DON'T FORGET

Listen carefully to the bass notes (i.e. the lowest notes). The bass note is often the root note of the chord.

DON'T FORGET

Listen out particularly for **chord VI** as this will always be a **minor** chord.

MUSIC GUIDE

In this question, you will be asked to identify features of a piece of music in the order they appear in the music. A guide to the music will be laid out for you to follow. An example of how this question looks can be seen below. You will see that further information is required and you should insert this in each of the four areas.

There will be a pause of one minute to allow you to read through the question.

The music will be played three times, with a pause of 20 seconds between playings.

In the first two playings, a voice will help guide you through the music (saying; '1 – 2 – 3 – 4' at the appropriate points in the music). There is no voice in the third playing.

1 The instrument playing the melody is a/an _____

2 A feature of the rhythm is _____

3 The music is in _____ time.

4 The melody features a descending _____

Course assessment – More on the question paper

Tips
- Follow the guide while the music is playing. Read the descriptions in the guide carefully. There is always a clue to the answer in the wording of the question.
- Pay particular attention to where the numbers are read out by the voice during the excerpt.
- Each answer you write must be a music concept.
- Sometimes the correct answer will be an Italian term.
- Sometimes there will be more than one possible answer.

MUSIC LITERACY

In this question you will be asked to answer questions relating to a section of printed music. An example of how this question looks can be seen below.

Listen carefully to the excerpt while you follow the music. You should not attempt to write during the first playing. Just familiarise yourself with the music. Remember that some of the notes or rhythms might be missing.

The music will then be played three more times with a pause of 30 seconds between playings.

After the final playing you will have 2 minutes in which to complete your answers. A warning tone will sound 30 seconds before the end of the question.

Here is an example of the format for the music literacy question.

You now have to answer questions relating to the guide score printed below. Listen to the excerpt and follow the music. Do not attempt to write during this playing.
The music will then be played three more times with a pause of 30 seconds between playings. After the final playing you will have 2 minutes in which to complete your answers. A warning tone will sound 30 seconds before the next question starts.

(a) Insert the time signature in the correct place.
(b) The rhythmic feature at the start is a/an _____.
(c) The notes in bar 5 form the chord of _____ major.
(d) Insert the missing notes in bar 7 using the rhythm provided.
(e) The interval bracketed in bar 11 is a _____.
(f) The cadence at the end of the excerpt is _____.

 DON'T FORGET

The **key signature** is at the very beginning, followed immediately by the **time signature**.

 DON'T FORGET

The key signature will be at the beginning of each line of music.

 DON'T FORGET

The time signature only goes at the beginning of the first line of music, immediately after the key signature.

 DON'T FORGET

The **tempo** indication goes above the stave at the first bar.

 DON'T FORGET

Dynamic markings go below the stave.

 DON'T FORGET

You may be asked to use appropriate Italian terms for tempo and dynamic markings.

 DON'T FORGET

You may be asked to insert missing notes or rhythms on the stave.

 VIDEO LINK

This example is from the beginning of the aria *Non più andrai* ('You shall go no more') from the opera *The Marriage of Figaro* by Mozart. Listen online at www.brightredbooks.net/N5Music

 ### THINGS TO DO AND THINK ABOUT

Make sure you know **how** to identify the key signature and the time signature; and **where** the time signature goes.

If you are asked to insert missing notes or rhythms, it is very likely that this will either be the same as, or very similar to, another phrase in the music. Look out for repeating patterns or **sequences**.

COURSE ASSESSMENT

MORE QUESTION STYLES

IDENTIFYING SEVERAL CONCEPTS

In this question you will hear an excerpt of music which will be played three times. You will be asked to identify **four** concepts; one from each of **four** different headings. The headings will vary from year to year, but may be any combination of the following:

style	rhythm	instruments
melody	tempo	timbre
harmony	texture/structure/form	dynamics.

You should tick **one** answer only in each of the four sections.

You will have 1 minute to read the question before hearing the excerpt.

The music will be played three times.

> **DON'T FORGET**
> Remember to tick **one** box from each section.

> **DON'T FORGET**
> If you are not sure of the correct answer(s) try to eliminate the incorrect concepts first.

> **DON'T FORGET**
> The headings will vary from year to year.

		Tick	
Melody	Sequence		Tick one box from this selection
	Countermelody		
	Descant		
Rhythm/tempo	Andante		Tick one box from this selection
	Cross rhythms		
	Compound time		
Timbre	Piccolo		Tick one box from this selection
	Con sordino		
	Distortion		
Style	Minimalist		Tick one box from this selection
	Celtic Rock		
	Pibroch		

INSERTING CONCEPTS IN A TEXT

In this question, you will be asked to describe music you hear by inserting the appropriate concepts in a given text. An example of this can be seen below.

There will be a pause of 30 seconds to allow you to read through the question.

You will hear the music **twice**, with a pause of 20 seconds between playings and 20 seconds before the next question starts.

> The music has _____ beats in each bar.
>
> The type of voice singing is a/an _____.
>
> The music is in _____ form.

IDENTIFYING PROMINENT FEATURES

In this question you will be asked to identify the **prominent** features of the music.

In your answer, you should comment on **at least three** of the following:

- rhythm/tempo
- melody/harmony
- instruments/voices
- dynamics (Italian terms).

contd

76

Course assessment – More question styles

You will hear the music three times, with a pause of 2 minutes at the end for you to complete your final answer.

You may use the table for rough working, but remember rough work will not be marked. The rough work table will look like this:

Rhythm/tempo	
Melody/harmony	*Rough Work*
Instruments/voices	
Dynamics (Italian terms)	

Make notes as you listen, in the rough work table.

Rough work will not be marked – only your final answer.

THE FINAL ANSWER

Your final answer must be written on the appropriate page, which will look like this:

Final Answer
_____
_____
_____
_____
_____
_____
_____

Remember to identify prominent features under at least three of the headings.

When writing your final answer you may choose any of the following approaches:

- writing your answers in sentences
- writing concepts as a list, or bullet points
- listing concepts under the headings provided.

DON'T FORGET

Avoid writing extensive lists of contradictory or unrelated concepts.

If writing lists of concepts, remember that the question is asking you to identify the **prominent** features of the music. It is important, therefore, not to write long lists of concepts unrelated to the music, or extensive lists of contradictory concepts. This approach would not be in the spirit of the question and may result in you incurring penalties.

If you choose to write concepts under headings, there will be no penalty for concepts being written under the incorrect headings. The important thing is to identify the correct prominent concepts. Remember that your rough work will not be marked. Marks will only be awarded for your final answer.

THINGS TO DO AND THINK ABOUT

Try to focus your listening on the most prominent features, and don't just list everything that you hear.

COURSE ASSESSMENT

COMPOSING ASSIGNMENT 1

OVERVIEW

The purpose of the composing assignment is to provide you with opportunities to explore and develop musical ideas to create music. The assignment has two parts:

- composing one piece of music
- reviewing the composing process.

Your composition may be in any style/genre and must last between a minimum of 1 minute and a maximum of 2½ minutes.

The submission of your composing assignment must include the following:

- an audio recording of your composition
- a score or performance plan of your composition
- a composing review.

The composing assignment assesses the following skills, knowledge and understanding:

- planning and reviewing your own music
- exploring and developing musical ideas
- creating music which is original to you.

In preparing your composing assignment it is important to note the following:

- An arrangement of your own or someone else's music is not acceptable.
- Your composition may contain sections of improvisation, but this must be in the context of a wider composition which demonstrates composing skills. A piece of music which is solely an improvisation is not acceptable.
- If you choose to work with pre-recorded loops this must also be done within the context of a wider composition and show the compositional process. Your own creative input must be clearly identifiable.

COMPOSING ASSIGNMENT TASK

For the composing assignment, you are required to:

- plan the assignment
- explore and develop musical ideas using at least three of the elements of melody, harmony, rhythm, timbre and structure
- create one complete piece of music.

So, during the process of working on your composing assignment you are encouraged to:

Plan – Explore – Develop – Create.

Plan

In planning your composing assignment you should:

- consider what kind of music you would like to create
- decide which instruments or voices you would like to use
- consider using a particular structure such as ABA, verse and chorus, or theme and variations
- make a note of your decisions.

contd

Course assessment – Composing assignment 1

Explore

In exploring ideas for your composing assignment you should:

- start with simple ideas – you can change or add to them later
- experiment with musical ideas using at least three of the following elements: melody, harmony, rhythm, timbre or structure
- reflect on your composing, considering which of your musical ideas are most effective
- make a note of your decisions.

Develop

In developing ideas for your composing assignment you might:

- change some of the musical ideas you have been exploring and experimenting with
- extend some of your musical ideas to make your composition more imaginative
- add more concepts or musical feature to make your composition more interesting
- make a note of your decisions.

Create

In creating for your final composition you should:

- decide which of your musical ideas work best
- use your best musical ideas to create your composition
- create a score or a performance plan for your composition
- create an audio recording of your composition
- make a note of your decisions.

 **DON'T FORGET**

Keep a record of decisions that you make so that you can come back to it for your composing review.

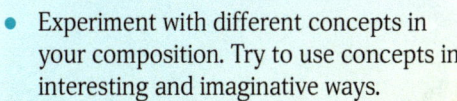 **THINGS TO DO AND THINK ABOUT**

- Consider composing for an instrument that you are familiar with. This means that the music you compose is more likely to be appropriate to the instrument.
- Consider experimenting with composing music in different styles or genres. Or, work within a style or genre that you particularly enjoy.
- Experiment with different concepts in your composition. Try to use concepts in interesting and imaginative ways.
- Remember to use your musical ideas in an organised way, so that your composition is coherent and musically convincing.

COURSE ASSESSMENT
COMPOSING ASSIGNMENT 2

SCORE OR PERFORMANCE PLAN

One of the requirements of your composing assignment is that you create either a score or a performance plan for your composition. A score would involve using your knowledge of music literacy to write down the appropriate notes and rhythms for your composition, using music notation.

Your score should include all the information required for someone else to be able to play or follow your composition. This would include:

- identifying any instrument(s) or voice(s) used
- notes written on the stave or staves
- key signature as appropriate
- rhythms and note values
- time signature
- bars and bar lines
- appropriate signs and symbols such as repeat signs or first and second time bars
- tempo indications
- dynamic markings as appropriate
- any other performance directions relevant to the instrument(s) or voice(s) used, such as arco, pizzicato, staccato, legato or accents.

Your score could be either handwritten, or printed using any music notation software.

If your composition makes use of improvisation, or is in a style or genre that does not lend itself to using standard music notation, you may decide to create a performance plan instead.

A performance plan is a visual representation of your composition that would clearly indicate what is happening in the music. Although a performance plan may not include any conventional music notation, it still needs to act a guide to the music. This means that the performance plan would need to clearly identify

- the overall structure of the music
- any instrument(s) or voice(s) used
- playing or performing techniques used by any instrument(s) or voice(s)
- concepts used in the composition
- how the concepts are used or combined
- any effects used, including electronic or digital effects
- any other features relevant to the music.

In identifying the overall structure of the music, you may refer to particular sections of your composition using headings such as

- Introduction
- Verse 1 / Section A
- Chorus / Section B
- Middle 8 / Section C
- Verse 2
- Chorus
- Coda.

If your composition has been created using a music application, rather than conventional instruments or voices, you may wish to include some screenshots in your performance plan. If you do include screenshots you must take care to explain what the screenshots represent in the music.

DON'T FORGET

Create a score or performance plan for your composition, as well as an audio recording.

DON'T FORGET

The score for your composing assignment needs to contain all the information required for someone else to perform or interpret your music.

ONLINE

You can also find music manuscript paper, with various templates, at www.brightredbooks.net/N5Music

DON'T FORGET

The performance plan for your composing assignment needs to contain all the information required for someone else to be able to follow what is happening in the music.

Course assessment – Composing assignment 2

AUDIO RECORDING

No matter what style or genre you have chosen for your composition, you are required to submit an audio recording so that whoever is assessing your composition can listen to it.

ONLINE

You can find a blank performance plan template, with guidance notes, at www.brightredbooks.net/N5Music

You may use any recording equipment available to you. However, in creating an audio recording of your composition, you must make sure that you choose an appropriate audio format for your final recording. You will need to be confident that anyone will be able to listen to your audio recording, irrespective of the device they are using to play it.

If you have used a specific music application to create your composition, you may need to export your work to a universal file type, such as MP3, so that anyone will be able to listen to it.

DON'T FORGET

Your composing assignment must have either a score or a performance plan, as well as an audio recording.

THINGS TO DO AND THINK ABOUT

Once you have created your final audio recording, try playing it on more than one device to make sure that it works.

COURSE ASSESSMENT

COMPOSING ASSIGNMENT 3

ASSESSMENT OF THE COMPOSING ASSIGNMENT

Your composition must use at least three of the following musical elements:

- melody
- rhythm
- structure.
- harmony
- timbre

The following table provides some examples of what a good composition might include, within each of these elements, as well as some common faults that you should be trying to avoid.

Musical element	What a good composition might include:	Some common faults to be avoided:
Melody	An interesting melodic shape, with a variety of steps and leaps.	A very repetitive or disjointed melody.
	Use of ornaments to enhance and develop the melody.	No melodic decoration or development.
	Show an understanding of scales or scale patterns (e.g. major, minor, whole-tone, chromatic or pentatonic).	Show little understanding of scales or scale patterns.
	Addition of a countermelody or descant to add interest.	Little evidence of a countermelody or descant.
	Using a variety of melodic devices such as question and answer, sequence, drone, pedal, inverted pedal or glissando.	A limited range of melodic devices, or over-using a particular melodic device.
Harmony	Using a variety of chords, including minor chords.	A limited range of chords.
	A chord progression that is interesting and convincing.	Inappropriate combination of chords.
	Using broken chord or arpeggio patterns to add interest.	Only using block chords.
	Use of modulation.	Little variety of keys.
	Using cadences in an appropriate and convincing way.	Showing little understanding of cadences.
Rhythm	Using a variety of rhythms and rhythmic grouping, including dotted rhythms.	Limited use of rhythms and little rhythmic variety.
	Using a variety of rhythmic devices such as anacrusis, syncopation, cross rhythms or rubato, in appropriate and convincing ways.	A limited range of rhythmic devices, or over-using a particular rhythmic device.
	Using different time signatures, including time signatures in both simple and compound time.	Keeping to the same time signature with little rhythmic interest.
Timbre	Using a variety of instruments or combining instrumental sounds in imaginative ways.	Using one instrument only, with little variety in tone or dynamics.
	Using a variety of playing techniques as appropriate to different instruments, e.g. arco and pizzicato strings, finger-picking and strumming the guitar, or using effects such as reverb or distortion.	Using a limited range of playing techniques, or not exploring the playing techniques possible on a particular instrument.
Structure	Organising your musical ideas in a systematic and convincing way.	Having musical ideas in a disjointed way with little sense of organisation.
	Using a specific type of structure such as ternary form, rondo form, verse and chorus or theme and variations.	Having no sense of a particular structure.
	Using a range of structural devices appropriate to the style such as ground bass, walking bass, Alberti bass, ostinato or imitation.	Using a limited range of structural devices or not using them in an appropriate way.
	Including structural features such as an introduction, contrasting sections, middle 8 or coda.	A limited range of structural features, displaying little contrast.
	Developing the music by using contrasting homophonic, polyphonic or contrapuntal textures.	Little contrast and limited use of different textures.

contd

Course assessment – Composing assignment 3

For the composing review, you are also required to:

- provide a detailed account of the main decisions you made when exploring and developing your musical ideas
- identify strengths and/or areas which may be improved.

The following table shows the different areas that will be used in assessing your composing review. It also provides a summary of what would be good to include in your composing review, as well as some common faults that you should be trying to avoid.

Composing review aspect	What a good composing review might include:	Some common faults to be avoided:
Main decisions made	A detailed account of the main decisions made.	A limited account of the main decisions made.
	A clear explanation of how you planned your composition.	Little evidence of planning.
Exploration and development of musical ideas	A detailed account of the exploration and development of musical ideas.	A limited explanation of the exploration and development of musical ideas.
	Identifying the concepts you have used in an organised way.	Simply listing concepts with little sense of organisation.
	Indicating how you have experimented with concepts and developed your musical ideas.	Little explanation as to how you have experimented with concepts or developed your musical ideas.
	Showing that you have considered different possibilities.	Little consideration given to different possibilities.
Strengths and/or areas for improvement	Clear identification of strengths and/or areas for improvement.	Limited identification of strengths and/or areas for improvement.
	Identifying clearly what works well in your composition.	Showing little understanding of what works well in your composition.
	Identifying clearly that you could do to improve your composition.	Showing little understanding of what you could do to improve your composition.

THINGS TO DO AND THINK ABOUT

A composing review template can be downloaded from the SQA National 5 Music subject page. However, you can also find a composing review template, with guidance notes, available at www.brightredbooks.net/N5Music

COURSE ASSESSMENT
COMPOSING ASSIGNMENT 4

MARKS

The composing assignment has 30 marks (scaled to 15% of the overall course award).

Marks are awarded as follows:

- composing music (20 marks)
- composing review (10 marks).

The following table shows a breakdown of the mark range from 0 to 20, along with the related composing summary statements, that will be used to assess your composing assignment.

Mark range	Composing assignment summary statements
18–20	An excellent composition demonstrating a range of musical ideas which have been developed imaginatively and convincingly — appropriate to your chosen style. The selection and use of elements is highly creative and effective.
15–17	A very good composition demonstrating a range of musical ideas which have been developed with some imagination — appropriate to your chosen style. The selection and use of elements shows creativity.
12–14	A good composition demonstrating a range of musical ideas which have been developed competently — appropriate to your chosen style. The selection and use of elements shows some creativity.
10–11	A composition demonstrating musical ideas which have been developed satisfactorily — appropriate to your chosen style. The selection and use of elements may be simplistic and straightforward.
7–9	A composition demonstrating musical ideas which have been developed inconsistently to your chosen style. The selection and use of elements is not always appropriate.
4–6	A composition demonstrating limited musical ideas with little development appropriate to your chosen style. The selection and use of elements is poor.
1–3	A composition which shows a very limited understanding of musical ideas with no development appropriate to your chosen style. The selection and use of elements is very poor.
0	No evidence.

Course assessment – Composing assignment 4

COMPOSING REVIEW

The composing review must include:

- main decisions made
- the exploration and development of musical ideas
- strengths and/or areas for improvement.

Your composing review can be presented in prose or bullet points and as a guide should be in the region of 200 to 300 words. The suggested word count is given simply to indicate the overall amount of evidence required. No penalty will be applied if you are outwith this word count.

The following table shows a breakdown of the mark range from 0 to 10, along with the related composing review summary statements, that will be used to assess your composing review.

Mark range	Composing assignment summary statements
9–10	The composing review contains: • a detailed account of the main decisions made • a detailed account of the exploration and development of musical ideas • clear details of strengths and/or areas for improvement.
7–8	The composing review contains: • a fairly detailed account of the main decisions made • relevant explanation of the exploration and development of musical ideas • identification of strengths and/or areas for improvement.
5–6	The composing review contains: • a satisfactory account of the main decisions made • sufficient explanation of the exploration and development of musical ideas • a satisfactory identification of strengths and/or areas for improvement.
3–4	The composing review contains: • a limited account of the main decisions made • limited explanation of the exploration and development of musical ideas • limited identification of strengths and/or areas for improvement.
1–2	The composing review contains: • a poor account of the main decisions made • a very limited explanation of the piece of music • little or no identification of strengths and/or areas for improvement.
0	No evidence produced.

DON'T FORGET

A composing review template can be downloaded from the SQA National 5 Music subject page.

ONLINE

You can also find a composing review template, with guidance notes, at www.brightredbooks.net/N5Music

THINGS TO DO AND THINK ABOUT

You must use the SQA composing review template which is available from the SQA National 5 Music subject page. However, you can also find a composing review template, with guidance notes, at www.brightredbooks.net/N5Music.

COURSE ASSESSMENT
PERFORMANCE 1

THE PERFORMANCE EXAM

The performance exam generally takes place in February or March, and involves you performing a programme of pieces on two instruments, or one instrument and voice, to a visiting assessor. The standard of music performed for National 5 should be no less than the equivalent of Grade 3 standard of other music examining bodies (for example, ABRSM, Trinity College, London College of Music, RCS Traditional Music Grade exams etc.).

The total length of your performing programme should be 8 minutes, and you should perform at least two contrasting pieces on each instrument, or voice. However, you can split the time of your programme any way you wish, so long as you perform at least 2 minutes on each instrument or voice. For example, you might decide to perform 4 minutes of music on each instrument. Or, you could perform 5 minutes on one and 3 minutes on the other, or 6 minutes on one and 2 minutes on the other. Just remember to make sure that you have 8 minutes in total. If you think your programme is going to be too short, you may have to consider including an extra piece or song. If your programme turns out to be too long, you may need to consider either cutting part of the music, or fading out, as appropriate. It is not necessary to make cuts unless your total performing time is going to exceed 8½ minutes, as there is some leeway allowed here. However, if you do need make cuts to any of your pieces you must make sure that you are not lowering the standard of the piece by cutting anything from the music that makes it easier to perform.

Instrumental and vocal performances should be accompanied as appropriate. Accompaniments may be live or pre-recorded. The use of pre-recorded accompaniments or commercially produced backing tracks is perfectly acceptable if they are stylistically appropriate.

DON'T FORGET

The total length of your performing programme should be 8 minutes.

Each piece that you play, or sing, will be marked out of 10, and then scaled to give a mark out of 30 for each instrument, or voice. This means that your two instruments, or one instrument and voice, will be worth a total of 60 marks. This mark will then be scaled to a mark out of 50, which means that the whole performance exam is worth 50% of the overall course.

Start to time your pieces. Think about how long your overall programme is going to last. Is your programme for one instrument going to be longer than the other, or will they both be the same length?

ACTIVITY

While it is not possible to provide detailed advice on preparing for the performing exam for every single instrument, the following general advice is offered for some of the most common instrumental and vocal categories.

Course assessment – Performance 1

KEYBOARD INSTRUMENTS

Much of the advice offered here applies to all keyboard instruments (e.g. piano, electronic keyboard, electronic organ, pipe organ and accordion).

- Performances on all keyboard instruments require the use of both right and left hands.
- Performances on the piano should pay attention to dynamics, phrasing and articulation, as appropriate.
- Performances on the electronic keyboard may use single-fingered or auto-chord facilities for the accompaniment.
- Performances on electronic keyboard or electronic organ may be enhanced by using changes of tone or registration, or the use of other effects such as fills, to provide variety to the sound.
- Electronic organ and pipe organ performances would also benefit from changes in registration, to vary the overall sound.

A printed copy of the music you are playing needs to be provided for the visiting assessor on the day of the exam.

Music for electronic keyboard would generally consist of a melody line with chord names printed either above or below the melody. You would be expected to play the melody line with your right hand and provide the chordal accompaniment with your left hand.

Music for accordion may consist of a melody line for right hand with chord names printed above or below the melody, or a fully notated left hand part. Either would be acceptable.

 **DON'T FORGET**

Performances on any keyboard instrument should include both right and left hands.

 ONLINE

Reflect on your performing progress by filling in the performance self-reflection sheet at www.brightredbooks.net/N5Music

 THINGS TO DO AND THINK ABOUT

If you are playing the electronic keyboard, or organ, consider changing tones or registration to vary the sound and enhance your performance.

COURSE ASSESSMENT
PERFORMANCE 2

GUITAR (ACOUSTIC AND ELECTRIC) AND UKULELE

Much of the advice offered for guitar also applies to bass guitar and ukulele.

Guitar programmes may be presented in any of the following different ways:

- A programme of pieces for chordal/rhythm guitar throughout.
- A programme of pieces for melodic/lead guitar throughout.
- A programme of pieces containing a mixture of chordal/rhythm and melodic/lead styles.

If a guitar programme is for chordal/rhythm guitar, or a mixture of chordal/rhythm and melodic/lead styles, the programme must still contain a minimum number of 12 different chords in the the performance. The chords should be played in a continuous accompanying style, which might include techniques such as strumming, finger-picking, arpeggiated chords, barré chords, or more complex playing techniques appropriate to different styles of music.

In the case of a chordal/rhythm guitar piece, you need to provide a printed copy of the melodic line that the guitar is accompanying, in standard music notation. This could simply be a copy of the melody line which the chordal guitar is accompanying, with the chord names printed above or below the melody. Guitar tablature on its own is not sufficient for examination purposes. Neither is a lyric sheet with only chord names and no music notation.

The melodic line also needs to be performed, as this provides the musical context for the performance. The melodic line can be performed by your teacher, another candidate or any other performer. It could also be pre-recorded.

If you are playing an electric guitar or bass guitar, you will have additional items of equipment to think about. As well as the instrument itself, which you will need to make sure is in tune, you will also need to make sure that you have an amplifier and a guitar lead. You may also be using an effects pedal and backing tracks. It is recommended that, before your exam, you take some time to make sure that everything you need is in full working order. It can be very unsettling to turn up for your performing exam, with your guitar and music all ready, to suddenly discover that your guitar lead isn't working, or there isn't an appropriate sound system to play your backing tracks. Here is a checklist for electric guitar and bass guitar players, to make sure that you have everything that you need for your exam.

Before the day of the exam:

- Check that your instrument is in working order and that the strings are in good condition. It may be a good idea to have a spare set of strings to hand, just in case any break on the day.
- Check that your amplifier is working properly, and that you know what settings will suit your performance.
- Check that your guitar lead is in working order. It's always a good idea to have a spare guitar lead, just in case something goes wrong on the day.
- If you are using any additional equipment, such as an effects pedal, make sure that everything is in working order and that you have all the necessary leads.
- If you are using backing tracks to play along with, think about what media you will use to play them. For example, will your backing tracks be on a CD, or will they be MP3 files played from a phone or a computer? You will need to make sure that an appropriate sound system is available for you to be able to play your backing tracks.

On the day of the exam:

- Do a final check to make sure that you have copies of the music you are playing, and all the equipment that you need.

DON'T FORGET

A guitar programme featuring chordal/rhythm guitar must contain a minimum number of 12 different chords.

DON'T FORGET

A copy of the sheet music for the piece you are playing needs to be available for the visiting assessor on the day of the exam. Guitar tablature on its own is not sufficient.

DON'T FORGET

If you are playing an electric guitar or bass guitar, make sure that both your amplifier and guitar lead are in good working order.

contd

Course assessment – Performance 2

- Make sure that all the equipment you are using, including your guitar lead, is working properly.
- Once you are set up, and ready to perform, take a minute or two to do a sound check, so that you have the correct balance in volume between your own instrument and your backing tracks. Firstly, make sure that you have the appropriate settings on your instrument, amplifier and any other equipment you will be using. Secondly, check the volume levels of any backing tracks that you are using. Make sure that the levels are suitable for both you and the visiting assessor to hear.

VOICE

As well as demonstrating both melodic and rhythmic accuracy, and attention to the same performance aspects as any other instrument, a successful vocal performance should also demonstrate very good diction and a strong sense of communicating the meaning of the song.

In certain genres of popular and traditional music, it may be appropriate to interpret the music with a certain degree of melodic or rhythmic freedom. Although this can be stylistically acceptable in certain types of music, you must be careful not to interpret the song so freely that it becomes an inaccurate performance.

Singers are recommended to perform from memory, as this tends to enable a more convincing interpretation and presentation of the song. However, performing from memory is not a mandatory requirement. If you do feel that you need to rely on having a copy of the words or music, it is suggested that you place your music neatly on a music stand, to avoid the copy of the music becoming a distraction to the performance.

Songs may be accompanied or unaccompanied, as appropriate, and transposed to any suitable key. Accompaniments may be performed on any appropriate instrument. The use of pre-recorded accompaniments or commercially produced backing tracks is perfectly acceptable if stylistically appropriate.

TUNED PERCUSSION

For performances on tuned percussion instruments, such as glockenspiel, xylophone or marimba, it is recommended that two beaters are used. While using two beaters is not a mandatory requirement, it is regarded as good practice. Although it is possible to play a piece perfectly accurately with just one beater, some pieces with melodic leaps and more complex rhythms may be difficult to perform properly without two beaters.

There are two percussion categories for SQA performing exams.

Category 1	Category 2
Drum kit	Tuned percussion:
Snare drum	Xylophone
Pipe band snare drum	Glockenspiel
Timpani	Marimba

If you select a tuned percussion instrument from Category 2, it is also possible to offer a separate programme on an instrument from Category 1, as these instruments are in different percussion categories.

> **DON'T FORGET**
> Accompaniments may be live or pre-recorded. The use of pre-recorded accompaniments or commercially produced backing tracks is perfectly acceptable if stylistically appropriate.

> **DON'T FORGET**
> Aim for good diction and a strong sense of communicating the meaning of the song.

> **DON'T FORGET**
> Tuned percussion pieces should be accompanied, unless a piece is specifically an unaccompanied study.

> **ONLINE**
> Reflect on your performing progress by filling in the performance self-reflection sheet at www.brightredbooks.net/N5Music

THINGS TO DO AND THINK ABOUT

- *Guitar:* Remember to include a variety of playing techniques such as strumming, finger-picking, arpeggiated chords and barré chords within your programme.
- *Voice:* Aim to perform your vocal programme from memory, as this enables a more convincing interpretation and presentation of the song.
- *Tuned percussion:* Try to use two beaters, alternating between left and right hands. This generally results in a more accurate and fluent performance.

COURSE ASSESSMENT
PERFORMANCE 3

DRUM KIT

For the National 5 Performing exam, you must select and perform a complete programme on one of the following: drum kit, snare drum, pipe band snare drum or timpani (see Category 1 in Tuned percussion, above). It is, therefore, possible to offer a programme on a second instrument from Category 2.

For performances on drum kit, you will be required to perform a programme of pieces demonstrating four contrasting styles. You should refer to the SQA Drum kit Style Bank (see next page), and select no more than one style from any four of the nine Style Banks. Each style must include four different fills, and must demonstrate four-way independence (i.e. using both hands and both feet).

Drum kit programmes must be accompanied, to provide a musical context for the performance. Accompaniments for drum kit programmes can be either live or pre-recorded. The use of pre-recorded accompaniments or commercially produced backing tracks is perfectly acceptable if stylistically appropriate. However, it is also acceptable for one drum kit piece only within the whole programme to be unaccompanied.

It is also possible, in a drum kit programme, to include two styles within the one piece (e.g. Rock and Disco). However, this is only permitted within one piece in the programme. In this case it would not be necessary to include double the number of fills.

Drum kit candidates should be aware that some commercially available drum kit publications, although produced for particular graded examinations, may not always contain the appropriate number of fills required for SQA examinations. If you use such publications you may need to include extra fills at appropriate places in the music in order to meet the SQA requirements. Such additional fills would need to be notated on the copy of the music.

DON'T FORGET

For National 5 Music you must perform four contrasting styles from four different Style Banks.

If your drum kit programme is too long, it is perfectly acceptable to make cuts, or fade out (in the case of backing-tracks) as appropriate, to keep within the time limit. However, if you do make cuts to the music, or fade out before the end, you must make sure that you are still including all the appropriate requirements in terms of styles, fills and four-way independence.

In selecting four contrasting styles, drum kit candidates should also be aware that some commercially available drum kit publications may contain pieces that don't necessarily relate to the rhythm style suggested in the title of the piece. For example, you might be playing a piece called *Bright Red Blues*, suggesting that the piece would in a **Blues** style (from Style Bank 3). However, although the piece may be based on a **Blues** chord progression, it might actually use a **Rock** rhythm (from Style Bank 1). It is very important, therefore, to makes sure that the four rhythm styles that you include in your drum kit programme all come from different Style Banks.

contd

Course assessment – Performance 3

SQA Drum kit Style Bank

Bank 1	Bank 2	Bank 3	Bank 4	Bank 5	Bank 6	Bank 7	Bank 8	Bank 9
Rock Heavy Rock Rock Ballad Metal Rock	Disco 16th note rhythm	Blues (3 quavers to one crotchet)	Shuffle	Jazz (2 or 4 feel)	Waltz	Reggae	Cha Cha	Irregular Time Signatures
Pop	16 beat	12/8	Funk shuffle	Swing	3 beats (simple or compound time)	Ska	Bossa Nova	Free choice of any other style not listed in Banks 1–8
Hip-hop Soul Hard Rock Punk Funk R'n'B Rock'n'roll				Big Band Swing	9/8		Latin Samba Rumba Calypso	

DON'T FORGET

A drum kit programme must contain four contrasting styles (from the Style Bank). Each style must include four different fills, and must demonstrate four-way independence.

ORCHESTRAL INSTRUMENTS

If you are playing an orchestral instrument, one important factor to keep in mind for your performance exam is to make sure that your instrument is properly in tune. It is perfectly acceptable to have your teacher tune the instrument for you.

While you may be playing an unaccompanied piece as part of your programme, such as an unaccompanied study, it is likely that most of your programme will require some form of accompaniment. The accompaniment may be live, played on the piano or some other instrument, or pre-recorded. You may use a commercially produced backing track for your accompaniment if this is stylistically appropriate. If your accompaniment is going to be live, make sure that you have adequate time to rehearse with your accompanist. It may be that your own instrumental teacher will accompany you, meaning that you will probably have had many opportunities to practise with the accompaniment in your lessons. However, if someone else is going to accompany you, it would be advisable for you to make arrangements with them, well in advance of the exam, to allow both of you adequate time to rehearse together.

DON'T FORGET

Make sure your instrument is in tune.

DON'T FORGET

Allow yourself plenty of time to rehearse with your accompanist.

ONLINE

Reflect on your performing progress by filling in the performance self-reflection sheet at www.brightredbooks.net/N5Music

THINGS TO DO AND THINK ABOUT

Is your backing/accompaniment going to be a live performance, pre-recorded backing tracks, or a mixture of both?

Make sure that you give yourself plenty of time to practise with the appropriate backing/accompaniment.

COURSE ASSESSMENT
PERFORMANCE 4

BAGPIPES

Highland bagpipes must be presented for the National 5 Music performing exam. A practice chanter would not be acceptable.

Bagpipe candidates are required to perform their bagpipe programme from memory. There is no requirement to play a March, Strathspey *and* Reel. The emphasis is on performing a varied programme of contrasting styles.

It is current practice for bagpipe candidates to be assessed by a specialist bagpipe visiting assessor. This means that your bagpipe performing exam will most likely be on a different day from the performing exam for your other instrument, or voice.

TRADITIONAL MUSIC PERFORMANCES

The general advice offered here is for instruments such as Scots fiddle, tin whistle, clarsach, accordion and voice, performing traditional music.

While a number of performers who play or sing traditional music learn a lot of their music *by ear*, it is still a requirement of the SQA performance exam that a copy of the printed music must be provided for the visiting assessor.

In many cases this shouldn't pose too much difficulty, as there are a number of publications of traditional songs and fiddle tunes that could be used for examination purposes. The Royal Conservatoire of Scotland also publishes a range of appropriate pieces for the Traditional Music Graded Exams.

If, however, you are performing a traditional tune that you do not have the sheet music for, you may need to create your own printed version of the melody. You could do this either by writing the melody out on manuscript paper, or by using music notation software to produce your own sheet music version of the piece. Even if you do have a copy of the sheet music you may be performing your own interpretation of the tune, or embellishing the melody. In this case it would be advisable to annotate your copy of the music to show exactly what you are doing.

As is the case with some styles of popular music, it can be acceptable to interpret some traditional tunes with a certain degree of melodic or rhythmic freedom. Although this can be stylistically appropriate, you must be careful not to interpret the piece so freely that it does not actually relate well to the printed music. In this case your performance may be regarded as inaccurate.

DON'T FORGET

Bagpipe candidates are required to perform their programme from memory.

DON'T FORGET

As with all styles of music, you will need to provide a printed copy of the music for the performance exam.

ONLINE

Reflect on your performing progress by filling in the performance self-reflection sheet at www.brightredbooks.net/N5Music

THINGS TO DO AND THINK ABOUT

- *Bagpipes:* There is no requirement to play a March, Strathspey *and* Reel. Consider performing a varied programme of contrasting styles.
- *Traditional music performances:* While it is stylistically acceptable to perform sets of traditional pieces (like Scots fiddle tunes) unaccompanied, it may be helpful to have a piano playing a vamp accompaniment. This can help to keep the tempo and flow appropriate and consistent. Make sure that you give yourself plenty of time to practise with the appropriate accompaniment.

Course assessment – Performance 4

ASSESSMENT OF PERFORMANCE

On the day of your performance exam a visiting assessor will listen to your full programme and mark each piece individually out of 10. In order to award you a mark, they will consider how well your overall performance of each piece relates to a number of performance aspects, as well as considering how well your performance meets the performance summary statements.

The following table shows the different performing aspects that will be used in assessing your performance of each piece. It also provides a summary of the criteria you should be aiming for within each performance aspect, as well as some common faults that you should be trying to avoid.

Performance aspect	Criteria that you should be aiming for:	Some common faults to be avoided:
Melodic accuracy/intonation	Notes performed correctly, as written in the music. Playing or singing in tune.	Notes not performed correctly according to the music. Playing or singing out of tune.
Rhythmic accuracy	Rhythms performed correctly, as written in the music.	Rhythms not performed correctly according to the music.
Tempo and flow	Keeping in time and performing fluently. Performing at an appropriate and consistent tempo. A musically convincing performance.	Not keeping properly in time. Some faltering or stumbling. Performing at an inappropriate or inconsistent tempo. Breaks in continuity.
Mood and character	Conveying the mood, character and style of the music appropriately. Communicating the meaning of the music or song effectively. Paying attention to musical details and expression.	Not conveying the mood, character or style of the music appropriately. Not communicating the meaning of the music or song effectively. Paying little or no attention to musical details or expression.
Tone	Producing a good tone. A confident, convincing and well-developed instrumental or vocal sound. On the keyboard: using different tones, fills or effects.	Tone quality not good. Little evidence of development or control of the instrumental or vocal sound. Not changing tone, or using other effects such as fills.
Dynamics	Paying attention to dynamic markings in the printed music. Varying the volume level.	Not observing dynamic markings in the music. No variation in volume.

The following table shows a breakdown of the mark range from 0 to 10, along with the related performance summary statements, that will be used to assess your performance:

Mark range	Performance summary statements
9–10	A convincing and stylish performance which demonstrates excellent technique.
7–8	A secure performance musically and technically.
5–6	A mainly accurate performance displaying effective technical and musical control.
3–4	An inconsistent performance lacking sufficient technical and/or musical skill to communicate the sense of the music.
0–2	A poor performance with little or no evidence of required technical and/or musical ability.

After each piece that you play has been marked out of 10, the individual marks are then scaled to give a mark out of 30 for each instrument. This means that your two instruments, or one instrument and voice, will be worth a total of 60 marks. This mark will then be scaled to a mark out of 50, which means that your whole performance exam is worth 50% of your overall course award.

THINGS TO DO AND THINK ABOUT

Consider a piece that you are currently playing or singing:
- Think about how your performing currently relates to the different performing aspects. Which of the performance summary statements would best describe your performance overall?
- Think about how well your performance would meet the criteria that you should be aiming for. What could you do to improve your performance?

GLOSSARY OF CONCEPTS

A

AB (N5) Two-part form. See **Binary**. Music in two sections: A then B. These sections may be repeated.

ABA (N4) Three-part form. See **Ternary**. Music in three sections: section A, then B, then back to A.

A cappella (N5) Unaccompanied singing.

Accelerando (N4) The tempo (speed) of the music gradually becomes faster.

Accent/Accented (N3) Notes which sound louder than others.

Accidental (N5) A sign in front of a note to change the pitch, e.g. a flat (♭), sharp (♯) or natural (♮). See the Music Literacy section for examples in music notation.

Accompanied (N3) Other instrument(s) or voice(s) playing along with the main melody.

Accordion (N3) An instrument with a keyboard played with the right hand and buttons (which play chords) pressed by the left hand. Often features in a **Scottish dance band**.

Acoustic guitar (N3) A guitar which does not require any amplification to produce sound. It is usually played by plucking or strumming the strings, or using a plectrum.

Adagio (N3) Italian tem for a slow tempo (speed).

African music (N4) Music from Africa, often featuring voices, percussion instruments and/or African drums.

Alberti bass (N5) A type of broken chord piano accompaniment played by the left hand where the notes of the chord are played in the pattern of low, high, middle, high. Classical composers such as Haydn and Mozart often used this in their piano music.

Allegro (N3) Italian term for a fast tempo (speed).

Alto (N4) The lowest female voice. Also known as contralto.

Anacrusis (N4) A note, or group of notes, that come before the first strong beat of a musical phrase, particularly at the start of a piece. Sometimes called an **upbeat**.

Andante (N4) Italian term for a walking speed (tempo). Generally regarded as a moderately slow speed.

Answer (N3) A short musical phrase that follows on from a **question** phrase.

Arco (N5) Instruction given to string players to play with the bow. This term might be given to players after a passage played **pizzicato** (plucked).

Aria (N5) A solo song in an **opera** or **musical**, usually with orchestral accompaniment.

Arpeggio (N4) Notes of a chord played one after the other.

Ascending (N3) Notes getting higher in pitch.

A tempo (N4) Italian term indicating that a piece of music should return to the original tempo (speed) after there has been a change.

Atonal (N5) Music with no sense of key (e.g. major or minor). It tends to use **discords** and is a feature of some twentieth-century music.

B

Backing vocals (N4) Singers who support the lead singer, usually by singing harmonies in the background. This is a common feature of **Pop** and **Rock** music.

Bagpipes (N3) A musical instrument associated with Scotland, consisting of a bag squeezed by the player's arm, a blowpipe with a double reed, and drones.

Baritone (N5) A male voice with a range that is higher than a bass and lower than a tenor.

Bar lines (N3) Vertical lines in music notation that separate bars of music. Each bar adds up to an equal number of beats. See also **double bar lines**.

Baroque (N4) A style of music composed during the period 1600–1750 approximately. Bach and Handel were two of the composers from this period. A popular instrument was the **harpsichord**.

Bass (N4) The lowest male singing voice.

Bass drum (N4) A large drum belonging to the percussion family.

Bass guitar (N4) A type of electric guitar that has only four strings, and plays low notes. A common feature of **Pop** and **Rock** music.

Bassoon (N5) The lowest of the four main instruments in the woodwind family.

Beat (N3) The basic pulse you hear in music. The pulse may be in groups of 2, 3 or 4 with a stress on the first beat in each group.

Binary / AB (N5). A form in which the music is made up of two sections, usually labelled A and B.

Blowing (N3) The sound produced by blowing into or across the mouthpiece of an instrument, e.g. woodwind or brass.

Blues (N3) A style of Black American folk music, developing from spirituals and work-songs. Blues music is often in 4/4 time and is often based on a 12-bar structure and on a scale where some of the notes are flattened.

Bodhrán (N5) A hand-held wooden drum, played with a wooden beater. A popular instrument in traditional music.

Bongo drums (N5) A pair of high-pitched drums, usually played with fingers and the palms of the player's hands. A popular feature of **Latin American** music.

Bothy ballad (N5) A folk-song, usually with several verses, from north-east Scotland, sung by men and telling a story of farming life.

Bowing (N3) The sound produced by drawing the bow across the strings of a stringed instrument, e.g. violin, viola or cello.

Brass (N3) A family of instruments made from metal with a mouthpiece and a bell, e.g. trumpet, French horn, trombone, tuba and euphonium.

Brass band (N4) A group of brass instruments and percussion.

Broken chord (N4) The notes of a chord being played separately.

C

Cadence (N5) Notes or chords at the end of a musical phrase. See also **perfect cadence** and **imperfect cadence**.

Cadenza (N4) A passage of music allowing the soloist to display their technical ability, either in singing or playing an instrument. Commonly found in the first movement of a **concerto**.

Canon (N3) Strict **imitation**. One part starts to play or sing a melody, then another part enters shortly afterwards with exactly the same melody. See also **round**.

Castanets (N5) Hand-held percussion instrument popular in Spanish music.

Cello (N4) An instrument belonging to the string family. It is slightly smaller and slightly higher in pitch than a double bass. It can be played with a bow (**arco**), or the strings can be plucked (**pizzicato**).

Celtic Rock (N5) A style of music that mixes Celtic folk or traditional music with rock music.

Change of key (N4) A move from one key to another. See **modulation**.

Choir (N3) A group of singers performing together.

Chord (N3) Two or more notes sounding together.

Chord change (N3) The point in a piece of music, or song, where the harmony changes from one chord to another.

Chord progression (N4) A series of chords in a piece of music or song. The three most common chords are built on the first, fourth and fifth notes of a major or minor scale. Chords I, IV and V are commonly found in a 12-bar Blues chord progression.

Chord progression (N5) A series of chords in a piece of music or song. In N5, chord progressions will use chords built on the first, fourth, fifth and sixth notes of a major or minor scale. Many popular songs use the **I, IV, VI, V** progression.

Chorus (N5) 1) A group of singers. 2) The music composed for a group of singers. 3) The repeating section between verses of a song.

Chromatic (N5) Notes which move by the interval of a semitone, e.g. C, C♯, D, D♯, E, F, F♯, G, G♯, A, A♯ and B.

Clarinet (N4) A woodwind instrument with a single reed.

Clarsach (N5) A small harp, popular in Celtic and traditional music.

Classical (N5) A style of music composed during the period 1750–1810 approximately. Important Classical composers were Haydn, Mozart and Beethoven. Many symphonies and concertos were composed in this style.

Cluster (N5) A group of notes next to one another sounding at the same time, creating a **discord**. Sometimes played on a keyboard instrument with the palm of the hand or even with the forearm. Used in some twentieth-century music.

Coda (N4) A section at the end of a piece of music, bringing the piece to a close. In music notation a coda is often indicated with the following sign:

𝄌

Compound time (N4) Each beat is divided into groups of three.

Compound time (N5) The beat is a dotted note which divides into three, e.g. 6/8 = two dotted crotchet beats in a bar and each beat can be divided into three quavers. Time signatures in **compound time** include 6/8, 9/8 and 12/8.

Concerto (N4) A piece of music for solo instrument and orchestra, e.g. a piano concerto is composed for piano and orchestra. A **concerto** is often in three movements.

Con sordino (N5) Italian term. Using a device that changes the sound of the instrument and reduces the volume. *Con sordino* means with mute. *Senza sordino* means without mute.

Contrapuntal (N5) A musical texture in which each of two or more parts have independent melodic interest. Similar in meaning to **polyphonic**.

Contrary motion (N5) When two melodic lines move in opposite directions, e.g. as one part ascends the other part descends.

Countermelody (N5) A second melody played along with the main melody.

Crescendo (N3) Italian term, sometimes abbreviated to **cresc**. The music gradually becomes louder. An opening hairpin sign can also be used in the printed music:

⟨

Cross rhythm (N5) Contrasting rhythms played at the same time or played with an unusual emphasis, e.g. 3 against 2.

Crotchet (N3) A note that lasts for 1 beat.

♩

Cymbals (N4) A percussion instrument, round in shape and made of metal.

D

Descending (N3) Notes getting lower in pitch.

Descant (N5) A vocal countermelody generally sung at a higher pitch than the main melody and providing an accompaniment. Commonly found in hymn tunes and Christmas carols.

Diminuendo (N3) Italian term, sometimes abbreviated to **dim**. The music gradually becomes quieter. A closing hairpin sign can also be used in the printed music:

⟩

Discord (N3) Two or more notes played together that clash. **Discords** are a common feature of **atonal** music.

Distortion (N4) An electronic effect used in **Rock** music to colour the sound of an electric guitar. It gives a *fuzzy* sound rather than the usual clean sound.

Dotted crotchet (N5) A note that last for 1½ beats.

♩.

Dotted minim (N3) A note that last for 3 beats.

𝅗𝅥.

Dotted quaver (N5) A note that last for ¾ of a beat.

♪

Dotted rhythm (N4) A long note followed by a shorter note, e.g. a dotted quaver followed by a semiquaver.

Double bar lines (N3) Two vertical lines in music notation that indicate the end of a piece of music, or the end of a section of music. See also **bar lines**.

Double bass (N4) The largest and lowest instrument of the string family. It can be played with a bow (**arco**), or the strings can be plucked (**pizzicato**).

Drone (N4) 1) A note, or notes, held or repeated in the bass. 2) The low-pitched pipes of a bagpipe which hold on single notes to accompany a melody.

Drum fill (N3) A rhythmic decoration played on a drum kit.

Drum kit (N3) A set of drums and cymbals often used in **Rock** music and **Pop** music.

E

Electric guitar (N3) A guitar that requires an electric amplifier to produce sound. Commonly used in **Rock** music and **Pop** music.

Episode (N5) A contrasting section in **rondo form**, that comes between playings of the main theme.

F

Faster (N3) The tempo (speed) increases.

Fiddle (N3) Another name for the **violin**, used in Scottish folk or traditional music.

Flat (N5) A sign in front of a note to lower the pitch by a semitone (♭). See also **Accidental**.

Flute (N4) A high-pitched instrument belonging to the woodwind family, although it is generally made of metal.

Flutter tonguing (N5) A method of producing sound in which the player rolls the letter 'r' while blowing into the instrument. It is used by wind players and is particularly effective for flute and brass.

94

Glossary of concepts

Folk group (N3) A group of two or more musicians who perform music in a traditional style, usually accompanied by guitars.

Forte (N3) Italian term meaning a loud volume. Sometimes abbreviated to **f**.

Fortissimo (N5) Italian term meaning very loud volume. Sometimes abbreviated to **ff**.

French horn (N5) An instrument belonging to the brass family, with a bell-shaped opening at one end and a mouthpiece at the other.

G

Gaelic psalms (N5) Unaccompanied Gaelic hymn tune, heard mostly in the Western Isles of Scotland. Usually led by a precentor with the congregation joining in.

Glissando (N5) Sliding from one note to another.

Glockenspiel (N4) A tuned percussion instrument from the percussion family. The metal bars are laid out in a similar pattern to the piano keyboard and are played with beaters.

Gospel (N5) Up-beat music with religious lyrics, often sung in praise or thanksgiving to God.

Grace note (N5) A type of ornament played as a short, 'crushed' note, before the main note of a melody. In music notation grace notes are usually printed in smaller type as a quaver with a diagonal line cutting through it.

Ground bass (N5) A theme in the bass which is repeated many times while the upper parts are varied.

Grouped semiquavers (N4) A group of semiquavers that are beamed together.

Guiro (N4) An instrument from the percussion family. It is made of wood that has been hollowed out and has ridges cut into the outer surface. A wooden stick is scraped along the ridges to produce the ratchet-like sound.

H

Harmony (N3) Two or more different notes played or sung at the same time.

Harp (N4) An instrument belonging to the string family. It has a large shaped frame and has 47 strings.

Harpsichord (N4) A keyboard instrument which looks like a small grand piano. The keys are laid out in the same way as on a piano but are opposite in colour. The sound is produced by the strings being plucked by quills. A popular instrument for **Baroque** music.

Hi-hat cymbals (N5) Part of a drum kit, consisting of two cymbals (one upside-down) that can be hit with a stick or brush, as well as being opened or closed with a foot pedal.

Homophonic (N5) A chordal texture where you hear the melody with an accompaniment, or where all the parts play, or sing, a similar rhythm at the same time.

I

Imitation (N4) When the melody in one part is copied a few notes later in a different part, overlapping the melody in the first part while it continues.

Imperfect cadence (N5) A cadence consists of two chords at the end of a phrase. In an **imperfect cadence** the last chord is chord V creating an 'unfinished' effect.

Improvisation (N3) When the performer makes up music during the actual performance. There may be suggested chords as a guide. **Improvisation** is an important feature of **Jazz**.

Indian music (N5) Music from India which uses instruments such as the **sitar** and **tabla**.

Inverted pedal (N5) A high-pitched note which is held on or repeated continuously, over changing chords.

J

Jazz (N3) A style of music created by black Americans in the early twentieth century. Related to **Blues** and **Swing**. Popular instruments in Jazz might include piano, double bass, drum kit, clarinet, saxophone, trumpet and trombone. **Improvisation** is an important feature of Jazz.

Jig (N4) A fast dance in **compound time**, e.g. 6/8, 9/8 or 12/8, in which each dotted crotchet beat is divided into three. Commonly found in Scottish traditional music.

K

Key signature (N5) Sharps or flats at the beginning of a piece of music to indicate the key of the music. The key signatures to be recognised are C major, G major, F major and A minor.

L

Latin American (N3) A style of dance music from South America. Percussion instruments provide lively **off-beat** dance rhythms.

Leap / leaping (N3) Moving up or down between notes which are not next to each other.

Legato (N3) Italian term for notes being played or sung smoothly.

Lines and spaces of the treble clef (N3) The system for writing music uses five lines and four spaces, each with a different letter name. The notes on the lines are called E, G, B, D and F and the notes in the spaces are called F, A, C and E.

M

Major (N4) Music in a major key or major tonality tends to use a number of major chords and major scale patterns, and is often described as sounding 'happy'.

March (N3) Music with a strong steady pulse with two or four beats in a bar.

Melismatic (N5) Vocal music in which several notes are sung to one syllable.

Mezzo forte (N4) Italian term for moderately loud volume. Abbreviation is **mf**.

Mezzo piano (N4) Italian term for moderately quiet volume. Abbreviation is **mp**.

Mezzo-soprano (N5) A female singer whose voice range is lower than that of a soprano but higher than an alto.

Middle 8 (N4) A section which provides a contrast to the opening section. It is usually eight bars long and is often found in popular styles of music

Minim (N3) A note that lasts for 2 beats.

Minimalist (N5) A style from the second half of the twentieth century based on simple rhythmic and melodic figures which are constantly repeated with very slight changes.

Minor (N4) Music in a minor key or minor tonality tends to use a number of minor chords and minor scale patterns, and is often described as sounding 'sad'.

Moderato (N5) An Italian term for a moderate or medium tempo (speed).

Modulation (N5) A change of key.

Mouth music (N4) A very rhythmical style of singing, with Gaelic or nonsense words, traditionally used for ceilidh dancing when no instruments were available.

Musical (N3) A musical play which has speaking, singing and dancing and is performed on a stage.

Muted (N4) Changing the sound of an instrument, by using a device to reduce the volume. See also **con sordino**.

N

Natural (N5) A sign in front of a note (♮) that cancels out a **flat** or a **sharp**. See **accidentals**.

O

Oboe (N5) An instrument belonging to the woodwind family. It uses a double reed which is placed between the lips and the air travels between the two reeds into the instrument.

Octave (N3) The distance of 8 notes e.g. from low C up to high C.

Off the beat (N3) Notes played on the weaker beats of a bar, e.g. beats 2 and 4 in a bar of 4/4 time.

On the beat (N3) Notes played on the stronger beats of a bar, e.g. beats 1 and 3 in a bar of 4/4 time.

Opera (N4) A drama set to music with soloists, chorus, acting, and orchestral accompaniment. It would include **arias** and **choruses**.

Orchestra (N3) A large group of instruments made up of four sections: **woodwind, brass, percussion** and **strings**.

Organ (N3) A keyboard instrument often found in churches. It usually has more than one keyboard, plus pedals that are played by the performer's feet.

Ornament (N4) A decoration to a melody by adding extra notes. Ornaments are often short and add melodic and rhythmic interest. See also **grace note** and **trill**.

Ostinato (N3) A short musical phrase or pattern repeated many times.

P

Paired quavers (N4) Two quavers (½ beat notes) beamed together.

Pan pipes (N4) Pipes of different sizes, made from bamboo, that are bound together. The sound is made by blowing across the top of the pipes. **Pan pipes** come from South America.

Pause (N3) A note, chord or rest that is held longer than written. In music notation, a pause sign can be written above the note, chord or rest to be held on.

Pedal (N4) Short for pedal point. A low note which is sustained, or repeated continuously, in the bass beneath changing harmonies. See also **inverted pedal**.

Pentatonic scale (N4) Any five-note scale. The most common one is that on which much traditional music is based, particularly Scottish and Celtic. Many Scottish tunes, such as *Auld Lang Syne* and *The Skye Boat Song*, are based on a **pentatonic scale**.

Percussion (N3) Instruments that are played by hitting, striking, shaking or scraping. Tuned percussion, e.g. **glockenspiel** and **xylophone**, can produce different notes. Untuned percussion instruments, e.g. **cymbals** and **triangle**, have no fixed pitches. See also **tuned percussion** and **untuned percussion**.

Perfect cadence (N5) A cadence consists of notes or chords at the end of a phrase. A **perfect cadence** is formed by chord V followed by chord I and sounds 'finished'.

Piano (dynamics) (N3) Italian term for quiet volume. Sometimes abbreviated to **p**.

Piano (instrument) (N3) A keyboard instrument which produces sounds by hammers hitting strings.

Pianissimo (N5) Italian term meaning very quiet volume, abbreviated to **pp**.

Pibroch (N5) Music for solo bagpipes, in **theme and variation** form, featuring **grace notes**.

Piccolo (N5) A half-size flute which plays an octave higher than the standard flute.

Pitch bend (N5) Changing the pitch of a note slightly, for example by pushing a guitar string upwards, or using a pitch bend wheel on an electronic keyboard or synthesiser.

Pizzicato (N5) An Italian term instructing string players to pluck the strings instead of using the bow, abbreviated to **pizz**.

Plucking (N3) A method of producing sound when the performer plucks the strings of a stringed instrument with their fingers. See **pizzicato**.

Polyphonic (N5) A musical texture in which each of two or more parts have independent melodic interest. Similar in meaning to **contrapuntal**.

Pop (N3) A style of music that is commercially successful and has been in the charts, either recently or in the past. **Pop** music tends to feature **vocals, electric guitars, drum kit** and **keyboards** and appeals to a wide range of listeners.

Pulse (N3) The basic beat in music. The pulse may be in groups of two, three or four with a stress on the first in each group.

Q

Quaver (N4) A note that lasts half a beat. See also **paired quavers**.

Question (N3) An opening phrase in a melody which is generally followed by an answering phrase.

R

Ragtime (N4) A style of music from early in the twentieth century, featuring a strongly **syncopated** melody against a steady **vamped** accompaniment. Often played on the piano. An important composer of **Ragtime** was Scott Joplin.

Rallentando (N4) An Italian term meaning the tempo (speed) of the music gradually slows down.

Rapping (N4) A style of popular music in which the performer speaks the lyrics in rhyme, generally to a regular beat. **Rapping** is popular in hip-hop music.

Recorder (N4) A simple woodwind instrument, often made from plastic or wood. There are four main types of recorder: descant, treble, tenor and bass.

Reel (N3) A fast Scottish dance in either 2/4 or 4/4 time. A **reel** generally features an even flowing rhythm and is usually played after a **strathspey**.

Reggae (N4) A style of popular music that originated in Jamaica in the late 1960s. It generally features a loud **bass** playing a **riff**, and a distinct rhythm featuring **accents** on the second and fourth beats of the bar.

GLOSSARY OF CONCEPTS

Repeat sign (N4) A sign in music notation (a double bar line with two dots) indicating that a section of music should be repeated.

When a section of music is repeated, but with a different ending, numbered brackets are placed above the appropriate bars indicating which ending to play the first time and which to play the second time. These are called first and second time bars. See Music Literacy section.

Repetition (N3) A musical phrase or idea that is played more than once.

Reverb (N5) An electronic effect which can give the impression of different hall acoustics, for example, as if the performance is recorded in a cathedral.

Riff (N3) A repeated musical phrase usually found in styles of popular music.

Ritardando (N5) An Italian term meaning the tempo (speed) of the music gradually slows down. Sometimes abbreviated to **rit**.

Rock (N3) A style of popular music is generally loud and has a heavy, driving beat. It usually features amplified instruments such as **electric guitars**, **bass guitar** and **keyboards**, as well as well as **drum kit** and vocals.

Rock'n'roll (N3) A style of popular music originating in America in the 1950s. It grew from the combined styles of **Jazz**, **Blues** and **Gospel**. Elvis Presley was an important Rock'n'roll performer.

Rolls (N5) A very fast repetition of a note on a percussion instrument, for example, on a snare drum or timpani.

Romantic (N4) A style of music from the period 1810–1900 approximately. Romantic music tends to be very expressive and contains a wide range of dynamics. The **orchestra** became much larger in the Romantic period, with the addition of more **woodwind**, **brass** and **percussion** instruments, such as the **piccolo**, **trombone** and **snare drum**, and an increase in the numbers of **string** players.

Rondo (ABACA) (N5) A form in which the first section (**A**) comes back between contrasting sections, called **episodes**. Section **A** would generally be in the tonic key, while the episodes are usually in related keys.

Round (N3) A musical form in which the same melody is repeated by other voices or instruments, entering one after the other before the original melody is finished. Examples of rounds include *London's Burning* and *Frère Jacques*.

Rubato (N5) An Italian term referring to some rhythmic freedom in a piece of music for expression, by slightly slowing down and speeding up the tempo.

S

Saxophone (N4) An instrument belonging to the woodwind family, although it is made from metal. It uses a single reed which is attached to a mouthpiece. A popular instrument in Jazz.

Scale (N4) A series of notes moving by step in either an ascending or descending order.

Scale (N5) For National 5 you may need to be able to recognise scales in the keys of C major, G major, F major and A minor. See the Music Literacy section.

Scat singing (N4) A type of vocal improvisation found in **Jazz**, often making use of nonsense words and meaningless syllables such as 'do-be-do-wap' or 'bop-she-wha'. Sometimes the singer imitates the sounds of instruments.

Scotch snap (N4) A very short accented note before a longer note, such as a semiquaver followed by a dotted quaver.

This is a characteristic of the **Strathspey**.

Scots ballad (N4) A Scottish song that tells a story, often about historical events, places or people associated with Scotland. Examples of Scots ballads include *The Braes O' Killiecrankie* and *The Massacre of Glencoe*.

Scottish (N3) Music which represents the various elements of Scottish music, for example, using Scottish dances, instruments associated with Scotland or songs or ballads about Scotland.

Scottish dance band (N3) A group of musicians playing instruments such as the fiddle, accordion, piano, bass and drum kit, for dancing. A Ceilidh band is sometimes known as a **Scottish dance band**. See also **vamp**.

Semibreve (N3) A note that lasts for four beats.

Semiquaver (N5) A note that lasts for a quarter of a beat. See also **grouped semiquavers**.

Semitone (N5) Half a tone, e.g. F to F♯ or B♭ to A. From one fret to the next on a guitar.

Sequence (N3) A melodic phrase which is immediately repeated at a higher or lower pitch.

Sforzando (N5) An Italian term indicating that a note or chord should be played with a forced sudden accent. Abbreviation **sfz**.

Sharp (N5) A sign in front of a note to raise the pitch by a semitone (♯). See also **accidentals**.

Simple time (N4) The music has two, three or four beats in each bar, and each beat can be divided into 2. Examples of simple time include 2/4, 3/4 and 4/4.

Sitar (N5) A stringed instrument from Northern India that is plucked using fingers or a plectrum. Melodies played on the sitar use special scales called *ragas* and rhythms called *talas*.

Slower (N3) The tempo (speed) decreases.

Snare drum (N4) An instrument belonging to the percussion family and is played with sticks or brushes. The snare drum can be found as part of a drum kit, as well as featuring in a pipe band.

Solo (N3) Music performed by one instrument or voice. A prominent instrument or voice can be solo even when accompanied by other instruments or voices.

Soprano (N5) The highest range of female voice.

Staccato (N3) Italian term for notes to be played short and detached.

Steel band (N3) A group of musicians who play music on steel drums (or pans). The top of each drum is hammered into panels to make different pitches. Steel band music is usually lively and energetic.

Step/stepwise (N3) Moving up or down between notes which are next to each other.

Strathspey (N4) A Scottish dance with four beats in a bar usually featuring **dotted rhythms** and **Scotch snaps**.

Striking (N3) A method of producing sound by hitting an instrument with beaters, sticks or hands.

Strings (N3) The family of instruments which have strings, e.g. violin, viola, cello and double bass. The sound is produced by drawing a bow across the strings or by plucking them with the fingers.

Strophic (N5) The structure of a song in which the same music is repeated for each verse.

Strumming (N3) A method of producing sound on a string instrument. Generally used by guitar players by drawing their fingers, or a plectrum, across the strings.

Swing (N4) A Jazz style of dance music that became popular in the 1930s and 1940s, and was performed by a big band. Common instruments include **saxophones**, **trumpets** and **trombones**, as well as **clarinets**, **piano**, **double bass** and **drum kit**.

Syllabic (N5) Vocal music where each syllable is given one note only.

Symphony (N5) A large piece of music for orchestra, usually in four movements.

Syncopation (N4) A rhythmic concept featuring strongly accented notes played on the weaker beats in a bar. Syncopation can be found in all kinds of music but is a common feature of **Ragtime**, **Jazz**, **Swing** and other styles of popular music.

T

Tabla (N5) Two small Indian drums tuned to different pitches and often used to accompany the **sitar**.

Tambourine (N4) A hand-held percussion instrument with a wooden or plastic frame and pairs of metal jingles. It is usually played by the performer's hand striking or shaking the instrument.

Tenor (N4) A high-pitched adult male voice.

Ternary (ABA) (N4) A form in which the music is made up of three sections, usually labelled A, B and A. Section **A** would be followed by section **B** (a contrasting section), then the music would return to section **A**.

Theme and variations (N4) The structure of a piece where a melody (the theme) is heard then returns several times with changes being made to either the melody or the accompaniment.

Time signatures in compound time (N5) The two numbers at the beginning of a piece of music. The beat is a dotted note which divides into three, e.g. 6/8 = two dotted crotchet beats in a bar and each beat can be divided into three quavers. Time signatures in compound time include 6/8, 9/8 and 12/8.

Time signatures in simple time (N4) The two numbers at the beginning of a piece of music. The top number tells you how many beats there are in each bar and the bottom number tells you what kind of beats they are. Examples of time signatures in simple time include 2/4, 3/4 and 4/4.

Timpani (N4) A large 'kettle' drum belonging to the percussion family. It was traditionally made from copper, with skin stretched across a large bowl. It is common to find timpani in the percussion section of an orchestra.

Tone (N5) The distance between two notes, equivalent to two semitones (for example, two frets on a guitar).

Triangle (N4) A percussion instrument which is a piece of metal in the shape of a triangle, open at one corner, and struck with a metal beater. It is an **untuned percussion** instrument, as it cannot play a range of notes.

Trill (N5) Moving quickly and repeatedly between two notes which are a step apart. In music notation you will often find the abbreviation *tr*.

Trombone (N4) An instrument belonging to the brass family. This is the only brass instrument that has a slide instead of valves.

Trumpet (N4) The smallest and highest instrument belonging to the brass family. The player uses valves to alter the pitch of the notes.

Tuba (N5) The largest and lowest brass instrument belonging to the brass family. The player uses valves to alter the pitch of the notes.

Tuned percussion (N3) Percussion instruments that can play notes of different pitches. Some of them can play full melodies. The most common are the **xylophone** and the **glockenspiel**.

U

Unaccompanied (N3) Music performed by a solo voice, a solo instrument, or a group of voices, with no other instrument or instruments playing in the background. Also called **a cappella**.

Unison (N3) Two or more performers singing or playing the same notes at the same pitch at the same time.

Untuned percussion (N3) Percussion instruments that do not play a specific notes or different pitches. Instead, they are used to add colour and texture to the music. Some of the most common are: **drum kit**, **snare drum**, **bass drum**, **cymbals**, **triangle**, **tambourine**, **guiro**, **castanets**, **hi-hat**, and **bongo drums**.

V

Vamp (N4) A rhythmic accompaniment with a bass note played by the left hand (**on the beat**) and a chord played by the right hand (**off the beat**). This is a common feature of Scottish dances played by a **Scottish dance band**.

Verse and chorus (N4) A structure/form used in many songs. The music of each **verse** will repeat, usually with different words. The **chorus** would have different music to the verses and generally comes in between the verses. A chorus, as well has having the same music each time it is repeated, would also have the same words.

Viola (N5) An instrument belonging to the string family. It is slightly bigger and lower in pitch than the violin, but looks similar. It can be played with a bow (**arco**), or the strings can be plucked (**pizzicato**).

Violin (N4) An instrument belonging to the string family. It is the smallest and highest pitched instrument in the string family. It can be played with a bow (**arco**), or the strings can be plucked (**pizzicato**).

Voice (N3) The sound produced by humans when they speak or sing.

W

Walking bass (N5) A bass line, usually played by the **double bass** or **bass guitar**, which moves mainly on every beat. A common feature of a variety of popular styles, including **Jazz** and **Swing**.

Waltz (N3) A dance with three beats in a bar in simple time.

Waulking song (N5) A style of singing by the women in the Western Isles of Scotland while they *waulked* woollen cloth to soften and shrink it. The songs are very rhythmic, with strong accents (to accompany the thumping of the tweed). Often the singing is led by a soloist with a response from the rest of the women.

Whole-tone scale (N5) A scale containing no semitones but built entirely on whole-tones.

Wind band (N4) A group of musicians playing a variety of **woodwind**, **brass** and **percussion** instruments.

Woodwind (N3) Instruments in which the sound is produced by the player **blowing** into, or across, the mouthpiece of the instrument, causing a column of air to vibrate. Most orchestras feature four woodwind instruments: **flute**, **oboe**, **clarinet** and **bassoon**.

X

Xylophone (N4) A tuned percussion instrument from the percussion family. The wooden bars are laid out in a similar pattern to the piano and are played with beaters.